West Hawai'i Parks

Museum Management Plan

Kaloko-Honokōhau

Pu'ukoholā Heiau

Pu'uhonua O Hōnaunau

Ala Kahakai

Pacific West Region/Seattle

February, 2004

West Hawai'i Parks

Museum Management Planning Team

Jonathan Bayless, Park Curator
Golden Gate National Recreation Area
San Francisco, California

Stanley C. Bond, Chief, Resources Management
Kaloko-Honokōhau National Historical Park
Kailua-Kona, Hawai'i

Kent Bush, Lead Curator
Pacific West Region/Seattle
Seattle, Washington
(Team Leader)

Mark Isaksen, Senior Curator
Northeast Museum Services Center
Philadelphia, Pennsylvania

Lynn Marie Mitchell, Archivist
Western Archeological and Conservation Center
Tucson, Arizona

Diane Nicholson, Special Projects Curator
Golden Gate National Recreation Area
San Francisco, California

Pacific West Region
National Park Service
Department of the Interior

West Hawai'i Parks
Museum Management Plan

February 2004

Recommended by:

Kent Bush   1.28.04

Kent Bush, Lead Curator
Columbia Cascades Support Office

Concurred by:

Geri Bell   2/20/04

Geraldine K. Bell, Superintendent
Kaloko-Honokōhau National Historic Park
Pu'uhonua O Hōnaunau National Historic Park

02/24/04

Daniel K. Kawaiaea, Jr., Superintendent
Pu'ukoholā Heiau National Historic Site

2/23/04

Aric Arakaki, Superintendent
Ala Kahakai National Historic Trail

Approved by:

03/03/04

Jonathan Jarvis, Regional Director
Pacific West Region

Executive Summary

The Museum Management Plan for the combined park units on the west coast of the island of Hawai'i identifies the museum management issues facing all the units, and presents recommendations to address these issues. A survey of the staff from all units was conducted to determine current informational and program support needs. A team of museum management professionals developed this plan in full cooperation with the staff responsible for managing individual park archives, museum collections, and library resources.

The combined units are responsible for managing collections totaling more than 428,000 individual items of cultural and natural significance that document the resources and history of the park units. These resources are in the form of archives, museum collections, and resource management library materials. More than 396,000 individual items are currently not cataloged. These resources are expected to grow significantly over the next decade with the use of the Service-wide Inventory and Monitoring Program.

Most of these materials are currently being stored under conditions that do not meet Service standards. These conditions include critical lack of space for storage and no space for access to the collections, thus compromising one of their primary values. Serious environmental control deficiencies (climate control and integrated pest management) affect the long term preservation of these resources. The remedial measures scheduled for FY2003 will provide some temporary relief, but no long term solutions.

Most of the documentation and preservation problems may be traced to the lack of a well-defined museum management program either individually or aggregately among all units. Professional support for museum management issues has been sporadic and fairly recent, and mostly from the staff at Hawai'i Volcanoes National Park on the east coast of the island of Hawai'i.

Summary of Recommendations

The combined units should consider several proactive steps for improving the museum management program:

- Combine administratively the collections from the four parks.

- Employ an experienced journeyman-level curator (GS-10) to provide needed program direction, and remedial and on-going management of the combined park collections.

- Connect the museum management program, using a role and function statement, to the records management, maintenance, and resource management programs in each park to assure the proper flow of information between the collections and users in the park.

- Partner with local organizations that have ties to the park units to ensure their concerns are heard and their various needs for information and use of the collections are addressed.

- Develop plans for a joint Cultural Heritage Facility for the preservation and use of the collections and records from all four units on the west coast of Hawai'i.

Table of Contents

List of Illustrations

Front cover   Herb Kawainui Kane: Voyagers (Ka'anapali 200 Years Ago),
1991,

                     (artist's collection)

Front cover inside   Sunset over Kaloko fishpond

Page 16, figure 1   Stone on which a checkers-like game, *könane*, was played, PUHO

Page 20, figure 2   *Ki'i* on beach at PUHO

Tables

Introduction

The Museum Management Plan (MMP) replaces the Collections Management Plan (CMP) referred to in the National Park Service publications *Outline for Planning Requirements* and *Cultural Resource Management Guidelines* and the *NPS Museum Handbook*. The CMP process generally followed an Operations Evaluation format, concentrating on the technical aspects of museum operations including a review of accession files, status of cataloging, adherence to guidelines, and resulting in detailed recommendations for corrections and improvements. As an approach to museum management planning, the MMP evaluates all aspects of museum-related programs within a park, and makes broad recommendations to guide development of park-specific programs that respond to the identified needs of the park.

The MMP recognizes that specific directions for the technical aspects of archival and collections management exist within the *NPS Museum Handbook* series; thus no attempt is made to duplicate that type of information in this plan. Instead, the MMP will place museum operations in a more holistic context within park operations by focusing on how various collections may used by park staff to support the mission goals of a particular park. This approach recognizes that there are many different ways that archives, libraries, and museum collections may be organized, linked, and used within individual parks, and it provides park specific advice on how this may be accomplished. Where required, technical recommendations not covered in the *NPS Museum Handbook* will appear as appendices to this plan.

In the case of the four parks on the west coast of the island of Hawai'i, the MMP was requested to assist with the development of a viable and multifaceted program that would support a joint operations scheme for the management of archives, libraries, and museum collections in support of individual park programs and the Ala Kahakai National Historic Trail. As a result, many elements of this particular plan are developmental in nature, and designed to guide the west coast units through the initial steps of creating a workable system that will support all aspects of joint and individual park operations.

To help with this process, the MMP Team surveyed staff from all of the parks to collect baseline data concerning archival and museum collections, the library, and various related services needed by the staff. The information collected allowed the team to make a quick evaluation of numerous factors affecting museum operations, and also provided valuable insights into how a well-designed museum management program might address the needs of park staffs.

The benefits, or outcomes, of an organized and administered archival and museum collections management program are often not well understood by parks. For that reason the potentials inherent in a well-developed program are often overlooked and under supported. Stated in the most basic terms—the museum management program should be designed to collect and preserve park specific data, and make that information available to park staff and the public in the most efficient manner possible.

Considered in this light, it is easier to understand how different types of resources in collections might be administered in different ways, depending upon the local needs for documentation, preservation, and use. This need for a unique, park-specific approach to the management of these resources is what the MMP process provides.

This Museum Management Plan was developed over a 12-day period from May 12 through May 23, 2003. The team became familiar with resources and operations of the four parks: Kaloko-Honokōhau,

Pu'ukoholāā Heiau, Pu'uhonua O Hōnaunau, and Ala Kahakai. Team members then developed, organized, and recorded the central issues and the necessary supporting information that comprises the plan. An out-brief was conducted with the park staff on May 22, 2003.

This plan is the result of team and park collaboration, including discussion and consensus, regarding all issues and recommendations. However, the plan was completed through individual contributions from Jonathan Bayless, Kent Bush, Mark Isaksen, Lynn Mitchell, and Diane Nicholson. The appendices were gathered from a body of suggested methodologies and reference materials generated over time by various NPS curators for other planning documents.

The team wishes to thank the staff of the west coast units, and in particular Stanley Bond, for the courtesy, consideration, and cooperation extended during this planning effort. The team also wishes to recognize the continued efforts and active participation of key staff from Hawai'i Volcanoes National Park, Laura Schuster, Keola Awong and Tracey Laqua, in providing continued professional assistance with the museum management program. The time, effort, and involvement of all these good people have been very much appreciated, and have served to make our job much easier. It is apparent that these individuals are dedicated and committed to the preservation of the park resources, and it is a pleasure to work with such professionals.

Figure 1   Stone on which checkers-like game was played, PUHO

Kaloko-Honokōhau National Historical Park

Introduction

Kaloko-Honokōhau National Historical Park (KAHO) was authorized in 1978 by Public Law 95-625 "to provide a center for the preservation, interpretation, and perpetuation of traditional native Hawaiian activities and culture, and to demonstrate historic land use patterns as well as provide needed resources for the education, enjoyment, and appreciation of such traditional native Hawaiian activities and culture by local residents and visitors…" Park collections, whether cultural, natural, or archival, are a tangible link to native Hawaiian cultural practices.

Collection Responsibilities

Initially, KAHO cultural and natural resource collections were a collateral duty of a park ranger. The first name to appear in ANCS is park ranger Victoria Steele in February of 1992. That same year these collections became the responsibility of the Resources Division under Laura Schuster. In 1999 Dr. Stanley Bond became Division Chief. The library collection, which includes some park reports and photographs, is still under the Ranger Division. Archival material generally falls under the division in which it was created. The Resource Division contains archeological and natural resource field notes and field maps, cultural and natural resource reports, oral histories, photographs, maps, specimen collecting permits, and GIS maps and data. Other divisions maintain their own archival files.

Cultural Resource Collections

KAHO is a relatively new addition to the National Park system and as such few archeological projects have taken place where artifacts were recovered. However, significant archeological excavations did take place within the Kaloko section of the park prior to congressional authorization. The purpose of this work was archeological survey, test excavation, and data recovery for the development of a resort community. These studies were carried out by Dr. Robert Renger and were eventually published by Dr. Ross Cordy (Cordy, Ross, et al. 1991. *An Ahupua'a Study: The 1971 Archaeological Work at Kaloko Ahupua'a North Kona, Hawaii*, National Park Service, Western Archeological and Conservation Center Publications in Anthropology No. 58). Most of the currently accessioned and cataloged material housed by the park, 655 objects, comes from this project. It is highly likely that other artifacts from this project have not been turned over to the park since some objects specifically mentioned in the report are not in the cataloged collection. Other objects in the collection come from the first phase of archeological research on Kaloko fishpond and randomly collected artifacts found by park staff in areas vulnerable to looting. Currently there are three archeologically recovered collections that have not been accessioned or cataloged:

• material recovered from archeological excavation and monitoring for the restoration of the Kaloko fishpond wall.

• material recovered from archeological monitoring during the stabilization of Aiopio fish trap.

• material from the archeological excavation of a midden site located in the south boundary road.

Park staff also continues to report and recover artifacts that can easily be looted. The location of each of these objects is mapped using GPS and entered into the park's GIS database. KAHO also houses part of the Pu'ukoholä Heiau (PUHE) collections. This material consists of archeologically recovered artifacts from the 1999 excavation of the John Young homestead.

Natural Resource Collections

Currently there are no accessioned or cataloged natural resource materials for KAHO. However, natural resource collections for the park do exist. From 1995 to 1997 Dr. Linda Pratt collected 243 botanical specimens from the park as part of a vegetation survey. This material is housed in the herbarium at Hawai'i Volcanoes National Park. In 2001 the park accepted materials collected by Dr. Marie Morin during her projects on Hawaiian stilts and coots found at Aimakapa fishpond. Most of this material consists of non-viable eggs. In May of 2000 the park buried a green sea turtle with plans to recover the skeletal remains.

Archival and Library Collections

KAHO contains a number of archival collections in the administrative, maintenance, ranger, and resource divisions that hold significant information about past park policies and activities. These include the material on the establishment of the park, records of the KAHO Advisory Commission, incident files, and records on the park's interaction with the Hawaii Land Use Commission. Perhaps the most important archival collection is the material collected by Linda Greene for her study, *A Cultural History of Three Traditional Hawaiian Sites on the Island of Hawai'i*, published by the NPS Denver Service Center in 1993. This document is now available on the NPS web site. Documents, photographs, and maps have been alphabetically filed and indexed, and are easily accessible to researchers. Other important archival materials include archeological and natural resource studies, oral histories, maps, and photographs, some of which have been accessioned into the library collection.

Figure 2   Two *ki'i* on the beach at PUHO

West Hawai'i Parks Museum Management
Plan

The basic principles for managing museum collections in national parks are not always well understood. Park managers, resource managers and interpreters are often too busy with their specialties and daily work to fully consider the concepts and logistics governing collections management. It is easy for parks to fall short of developing a sound museum management program and, as a result, not realize the full benefit and value from their collections.

This section provides the following background information about museum collections:

- The purpose of museum collections.

- How museum collections represent a park's resources.

- Determining where to locate museum collections.

- Establishing access, use and management policies for museum collections.

Purpose of Museum Collections within National Parks

Museum collections contain objects and specimens, and most museums administer their own archives and operate their own libraries. These functions are necessary to support the work of the organization as a whole. It is not unusual for these resources—archives, collections, and libraries—to also be accessible to the public.

Within national parks, museum collections (including archives) serve four basic functions:

- **Documentation of resources.** Park collections should serve as documentation of the physical resources of the park as well as the history of the park's efforts to preserve and protect those resources.

- **Physical preservation and protection of resources.** Park collections should help preserve and protect a park's resources, not only by keeping the specimens and collections made to document the resources, but also by preserving information about the individual items and the resource as a whole. This is central to the management of both natural and cultural material.

- **Research.** During documentation of collections, a park performs research to provide the background information used in cataloging. The park is also responsible for making this collections information available to legitimate research, which can itself lead to new discoveries about an individual item, or the park as a whole.

- **Public programs.** The park is responsible for using its collections to provide information to the public. Exhibits and publications are two traditional means of supplying public programs, but new technology has led to other communication methods, including electronic access through Web sites and online databases.

How Collections Represent a Park's Resources

A park's museum, library, and archival collections provide different perspectives on its resources:

- Museum collections, which contain three-dimensional objects and specimens, should represent the resources within the park boundaries. Examples of museum collections include: artifacts from archeological compliance activities; specimens and resulting reports from resource management projects; paint samples and building fragments from restoration of historic structures.

- The park archives may contain files, manuscripts, maps, building plans, and photos that document the history of park development and the management of its resources. Individual collections within the archives should further document the activities that created portions of the museum collections. Examples of park archives include: copies of field journals and maps created while collecting botanical specimens; photographs taken during historic structure work; maps and as-built drawings made during utility installation; and property, land, and water use agreements that document past acquisition and use of park lands.

- The park library contains both published literature and less formal reports and documents relevant to the park's resources and their management. Examples might include: general literature concerning local history, flora and fauna; specialized scientific studies involving biota and archeological resources found in the park; circulating copies of park specific planning documents; trade, craft and professional journals reflecting the need for park staff to remain current in their field.

Determining Where to Locate Park Collections

The *NPS Museum Handbook* should be used as a guideline for identifying locations for branch or satellite park collections, and establishing methodologies for their documentation, organization, storage, and use.

It is often most effective if collections are located centrally, as this promotes efficient use of space (particularly in terms of combining preparation and work areas). However, it may also be operationally efficient to split the collections among potential users (for example, the herbarium and insect collection going to Natural Resources for storage and use).

Branch or satellite collections are possible as long as proper preservation and security conditions are met, and the requisite work areas necessary for management and use are provided. Overall responsibility for documentation, preservation, and reporting should, however, remain vested in one curatorial lead position, no matter where branch collections are located.

Establishing Access, Use, and Management Policies

Access, use, and management policies define who can access the collections (both staff and public), what types of use are possible and under what conditions, and how the collections should be managed. Desired outcomes or products should be identified as well; for example, the type of services that are expected from the collections. Some examples include production of over-lays for buried utilities; production of

CDs containing research done at the park; liberal access to botanical specimens for comparative studies; and inter-library loan services.

Samples of access, use, and management policies are contained in the appendices to this plan. Note that these sample policies are generic—the park is encouraged to change and adapt them to fit park-specific needs.

The park may wish to consider the use of focus group exercises to develop a number of park-specific documents, including a Role and Function Statement, for the combined collections. These would clearly state who is responsible for the development of a joint resource and how the museum program will function to serve park-wide goals. Access and use policies should be defined and implemented, and responsibilities for development, documentation, and management of the resource should be defined in a formal position description and associated performance standards. These objectives must be fully defined in writing if they are to be accomplished in fact.

Some recommendations to consider for developing and formalizing the park's management philosophy for archives, libraries, and museum collections are as follows:

• Create a focus group of senior staff representing all park administrative units to define what the collections should contain, how they should be managed and accessed most efficiently, and what products should be produced upon request.

• Define the role and function of the combined collections by formal statement, formal access policies, and formal methodologies for depositing collections material, archival information and required literature into the collections.

• Assign responsibility for developing and managing the joint collections to a single administrative unit and individual using a written position description and performance standards.

• Identify possible cooperative partnerships in the community with groups that hold common interests regarding the preservation and management of park resources.

Figure 3   Depiction of ancient Kaloko fishpond by Hawaiian artist Herb Kane

Issue A —
Staffing, Planning, and Programming

Issue Statement

A professional staff and adequate planning, programming, and funding are required for the implementation of a successful museum management program.

Background

Park collections management within the four west Hawai'i parks dates from the authorization of Pu'uhonua O Hōnaunau National Historical Park (PUHO) in 1955. For a period after the authorization of Pu'ukoholā Heiau National Historic Site (PUHE), the two park units were jointly administered. With the authorization of Kaloko-Honokōhau National Historical Park (KAHO) in 1978, the Western Region decided to provide individual leadership and independent program direction for each park.

After the recent retirement of the KAHO Superintendent in 1997, it was decided to place this unit under the superintendent of PUHO. At the time of the site visit for this plan, three separate park operations were under the management of two superintendents. These parks are now reconnected by the Ala Kahakai National Historic Trail (ALKA), authorized by Congress in November, 2000. The superintendent and staff for the ALKA Trail are independent, but located with the KAHO offices.

The parks are spaced roughly equidistant along about 65 miles of the west coast of the island of Hawai'i. They are connected now (as they were prehistorically) by a trail that extends well beyond the current boundaries of the parks. All four park sites represent roughly the same ecosystem and life zones; they all provide critical habitat for threatened and endangered species; and they all represent the same developmental periods of Hawaiian culture. Three parks contain sacred sites and settlement areas, and all four units have direct association with Kamehameha, the prime mover in the unification of the Hawaiian Islands into a single political entity. Collectively the units provide an unparalleled opportunity to preserve, study, and illustrate Hawaiian culture as it existed from ancient times through the reign of Kamehameha I.

From the authorization of Pu'uhonua O Hönaunau in 1955, material has been entering the museum collections. The four parks together hold an estimated 438,603 individual items, of which an estimated 396,292 remain to be cataloged (see Table 1, page 37). Most of these resources are archival and archeological in nature, and are specific to the parks they document. A much smaller percentage of the collections represent the natural science resources of the parks, but this segment of the collections will increase dramatically over the next decade as a result of the Inventory and Monitoring projects for the four parks.

Collections storage is substandard in all four parks. There is currently no space for collections access and use in the four parks, and the improvements scheduled for PUHO and PUHE in FY2003 will only provide additional storage space—not sufficient room for the access and work functions required by collections.

None of the four parks has had a professional level curator on the permanent staff. Professional services have been sporadic, fairly recent, and mostly tied to the larger projects such as the John Young homestead preservation efforts. The lack of professional oversight is evident in the minimal museum registration (accession and catalog) for all four parks (see Issue B). Collection Management Plans were done for both Pu'uhonua O Hönaunau and Pu'ukoholä Heiau in 1989, but were never fully implemented. Draft Scope of Collection Statements were done for three parks in 1997, but were never finalized and signed by the parks. Lack of professional oversight is also evident in the poor storage organization, lack of basic planning documents, and the lack of an organized museum management program in any of the parks.

Discussion

Together, the four parks are responsible for a complex, diverse collection of over half a million items that document primary park resources. The Ala Kahakai National Historic Trail is expected to generate substantial archival resources, and additional archeological material may be offered from private collections as a result of this project. All factors considered, the combined collections of the four units could be expected to number over one million items within the next decade. It is critical to begin planning for the actions necessary to ensure the documentation, preservation, and access needs of these resources are addressed.

A fully functioning museum management program is more than just adequate registration and the safe storage of collections. Collections are not of any use to the park unless they play active roles in providing information concerning the park resources, and the efforts of park staff's management and preservation of those resources. Getting information into the collections (in the form of both objects and associated data) is only part of the museum management function; getting the information back out of the collections to answer a variety of staff and public needs is just as important. It is this aspect of "use" that is probably least understood, and is most often what is missing in the development of park collections management philosophy.

A defined professional approach to the management of these resources, either individually or collectively, is lacking for the west Hawai'i parks. The parks have been attempting individual management of these resources for over 25 years, and those individual approaches have clearly not been working for a number of reasons—principally due to lack of staff, lack of space, and lack of funding. The parks are also lacking the most basic ingredient to museum program development, the concept of what role and function the collections should play in the overall management of the parks. Given that the cultural and natural resources in all the collections are so similar in scope, content, size, and stage of development, it would be logical to have a role and function statement that would embrace all three units.

When documenting such a conceptual role and function statement for the museum management program (what is to be collected, where it is to be maintained, how it is to be used, who is responsible), input from each administrative unit (division, branch) within each park is necessary. Each park and administrative unit will have a unique view of the resources within its sphere of influence, and thus unique views of the kinds of things these collections need to contain and be made available for use. For example, maintenance may need utility maps during normal working hours. Resource management may need access to comparative collections to fit flextime schedules, and administration may need access to land and water files on a compact disk for use on the office computer. Filling all these types of needs is possible, but only if the collections are created and maintained with these types of outcomes in mind.

In addition, the parks should involve the local partnership organizations in an effort to determine what types of access and services these organizations may need. Conflicts of philosophy regarding the composition, preservation, and use of the park collections must be expected. It is important to provide a venue where these differences may be openly and honestly expressed, and fully considered. The collections contain potentially sensitive cultural material that could elicit varied opinions concerning possession, preservation and use. Perhaps many of the expressed needs for information and use can be addressed without adverse effect on the collections or Service policy. The parks may wish to involve regional staff in responding to some situations, and all decisions should be documented in a standard operating procedure specific to these collections.

The west Hawai'i parks are also lacking an individual or a collective approach to documenting the needs of each park's collections. There are scattered Project Management Information System (PMIS) project requests from each park, but no unified approach to solving the long-term problems of museum collections. Also, no Operation Formulation System (OFS) request exists for the necessary professional staff to manage the park collections, either on an individual or aggregate basis.

This lack of professional staff can be likened to a key part missing from a puzzle. Without the professional expertise necessary to define the role and function of the collections, produce the collections registration, perform the physical organization, assure the preservation, provide the access and information upon request, and document planning and budget needs, there is no program of organized care and use of these resources. Individuals without the necessary academic education and practical experience cannot perform work of this nature and complexity. This approach has not worked for the west Hawai'i parks for the past 20 years, and will not work in the future. For collections of this size and complexity, the services of a GS-1015/11 curator would be a minimal requirement.

Considering the above information, it is obvious that the individual parks under consideration in this plan lack both the professional expertise and the funding necessary to address the situation on an individual park basis. A centralized approach to a joint museum management program that will address the needs of all three park units, plus the historic trail, is required. While the vision for such a joint venture should encompass the concept of a joint work/storage/use facility, the realization of that objective is realistically at FY2008 or beyond. Development of a centralized museum management program should not wait for the development of the joint facility.

It is currently possible to start the process of centralization or joint management of these resources on an administrative level. The superintendents and staff involved just have to agree to make it happen. The second step is providing professional staff to perform the necessary collections registration and preservation, and to begin the planning and budget building necessary to basic program development.

In the short term it would be possible to "rent" these services from the staff at Hawai'i Volcanoes. The $3,000. add-on to each individual park budget for the ANCS+ catalog program and "associated" costs could be used to cover the costs of this assistance. Additional funds could be gleaned from the projects creating the collections, and/or from Backlog Catalog (BAC-CAT) projects for the individual parks. In addition, having the services of a GS-10 curator for project oversight is now a requirement for receiving BAC-CAT funding from the region, so having the system in place would facilitate this requirement.

An additional step for centralization would be the assembly of the accession documentation for all four parks in a central location. Review of the accession books and files from the four parks show minimal use of these documents, indicating the necessary documentation is not taking place even with the records available in the parks. Centralization of the accession books and related files would enable the curator of record to efficiently accomplish the necessary work without having to visit each park.

Recommendations

- Consolidate administratively the museum management program for the four parks on the west coast of Hawai'i.

- Formulate a focus group representing each administrative branch from each park unit, to define the products the individual units will require from the consolidated museum management program.

- Formulate a focus group representing the diverse community organizations to determine what types of access and services they may require from the consolidated museum management program.

- Develop a Role and Functions Statement from focus group results to guide the development of a jointly managed museum management program for the units on the west coast of Hawai'i.

- Contract with Hawai'i Volcanoes National Park to provide basic curatorial services (registration and preservation) for the joint collections in the short term.

- Contract with Hawai'i Volcanoes National Park to develop the basic documentation and funding requests (Collection Management Reports, Museum Collection Protection and Preservation Checklist, Scope of Collections Statements, PMIS Statements, Operation Formulation System Request) required to support the joint museum management program at the professional level.

Figure 4   Honoköhau Church Makai, ca. 1915, Hawaiian Mission
Children's Society

Issue B —
Museum Documentation

Issue Statement

The four Hawaiian parks need access to professional staff and updated museum records to ensure the highest quality documentation supports park operations and pubic access to collections.

Background

Museum documentation provides the record of ownership and detailed descriptions of the artifacts, specimens, and archives that make up park museum and archive collections. Documentation begins with the accessioning process, where collections are first made museum property, and consists of the accession book, accession files (containing the vital Accession Receiving Report and possibly the List of Objects, Deed of Gift, purchase document, Receipt for Property, and other documents related to the acquisition), and an accession database record in the Automated National Catalog System (ANCS+). Specific information about individual artifacts or groups of similar artifacts is contained in the catalog record, which is entered into the ANCS+ database. If additional documents such as physical photographs and treatment reports exist for cataloged objects, they are placed in catalog folders.

An annual inventory of collections is completed to provide accountability and help ensure against losses. The Checklist for the Preservation and Protection of Museum Collections documents how parks meet the standards for museum facilities and operations; it is completed every other year. Archives can generate additional documentation unique to the archives discipline, including container lists and finding aids (see

Issue C on archival collections). The Scope of Collection Statement, although not considered technically part of museum documentation, will be addressed in this issue because of its important role in guiding new acquisitions.

Three of the park units covered by this plan, Pu'uhonua O Hōnaunau (PUHO), Kaloko-Honokōhau (KAHO), and Pu'ukoholā Heiau (PUHE), share certain elements common to the management of their museum documentation. These parks have had collateral duty curators since their inceptions, and have relied on professional curatorial assistance to complete some of their accessions. NPS museum staff on temporary details have completed much of the cataloging, and some of these need to be updated. The overwhelming majority of collections consist of archeological and archival materials. Most of the recent organization and documentation of the park archives is the result of project activities.

Two Collection Management Plans were completed for PUHO and PUHE in 1989, based on site visits conducted in 1984. The plans state that in 1987 there was no backlog of accessions or cataloging. This was due to the efforts of NPS curators from the Western Regional Office and Yosemite National Park who completed the accession records and cataloged all artifacts to the basic registration level, the minimum amount of information necessary to generate a catalog record. This approach is no longer encouraged, since rarely does cataloging get revised once entered. As a case in point, 15 years have passed without the opportunity available to update the 1987 catalog records.

The current museum collection summaries for each park are given in Table 1, based on the 2002 Collections Management Report (CMR) and does not include current un-accessioned materials. There are about 600 un-accessioned biological specimens currently stored at Hawai'i Volcanoes National Park, consisting of 200 invertebrates and 400 herbarium specimens. There are an estimated 150,000 pages of archives from PUHO waiting to be accessioned. The earlier preponderance of archeological collections has been overtaken by large numbers of recent archival additions.

Table 1: West Hawai'i park collections according to FY2002 Collections Management Report

PARK	ARCH- EOLOGY	ETHNO- LOGY	HISTORY	ARCHIVES	BIOLOGY	TOTAL
KAHO	656			264,000	243	264,899
PUHE	1,023	3	224	16	35	1,301
PUHO	16,208		25	146,060	10	162,303
ALKA				10,100		10,100
TOTAL	17,887	3	249	420,176	288	438,603

The similarities of the collections types and the museum documentation needs of the four parks, along with their relatively close geographic proximity, allow for the consideration of joint solutions to problem solving. This is the approach taken in the past and it is still valid today.

Discussion

Many of the accession records at the parks do not meet NPS standards, and need updating and corrections to fully achieve museum quality records.

At PUHO some 82 accessions have been created but only 70 have accession file folders, and these are maintained within the collections storage room. The ANCS+ database is contained on the computer located in the office of the Chief of Cultural Resources. Many of the entries need improvements in the names, titles, and addresses of the source of accessions, and inventories of objects contained within each accession. Include the name (last name first) and complete address for outside people, and full name, title, and park or office for NPS staff.

At PUHE there are 17 accessions in the accession book and 17 accession folders. At KAHO there are nine accessions and nine accession files located within the Bally Building. These records are located within the collections storage room, as well as the laptop computer that contains the ANCS+ database.

For all the parks, there must be one file for every accession, and each needs to contain all the necessary documentation of the accession as legal proof of government ownership and identity. All the documentation — any information that provides insight into the materials, why they are in the collection, and the appropriate legal documentation such as Deed of Gift, Loan Agreement, or Receipt for Property—must be put into the folder. Names, titles, and addresses must be noted on the Accession Receiving Report, including those of NPS staff members for field collections. In the future, archeological collections received from archeologists should include documentation from the land owner(s) indicating the archeologist either has title to the materials or has the right to dispose of the materials.

Accessioning the backlog of objects and archives is critical to getting these materials listed on the CMR and achieving official status for budgeting and programming purposes. Updating these records and eliminating backlog and deficiencies must be completed by staff who are fully trained and experienced with NPS museum documentation standards. On the island of Hawai'i, only Hawai'i Volcanoes National Park has such staff available, and they have acted as the curator of record in the past. It is recommended that the west Hawai'i parks enter into an agreement with HAVO to obtain curatorial services every one to three months for the purposes of updating the museum accession records. To ensure their consistency and protection against loss or damage, these accession books and files from PUHO and PUHE should be stored at KAHO, which has the most secure museum storage room. Copies of these files would remain at the parks for reference use, and all new accessions would be directed to the curator of record for processing at KAHO.

Catalog records exhibit a wide diversity of completeness and quality, and will require a greater investment in staff time and expertise to update. At PUHO basic registration exists for most objects, but many of these records are in need of substantial research and description of the materials they cover. The recent work performed on archival cataloging (three catalog records containing some 15,100 documents) was not submitted to the National Catalog in time to be added to the 2002 CMR. At KAHO the catalog records are mostly complete, and while some could use updating, they come close to meeting the standards of being fully cataloged. At PUHE, the John Young house site archeological catalog records contain accurate and complete information, but a number of the earlier records need help. The backlog of cataloging needs to be eliminated through submittal of funding requests to the annual budget call (see Issue A on programming). Backup copies of the ANCS+ database for accessions and catalog records should be placed at KAHO as a method of data protection and one that would provide centralized access to the curator of record.

Compliance with the Native American Graves and Repatriation Act (NAGPRA) is an important component of the museum documentation for the three parks which contain numerous burial and sacred native Hawaiian sites. The mandate of these parks is similar to that stated for KAHO: "...to provide a center for the preservation, interpretation, and perpetuation of traditional native Hawaiian activities and culture..." Repatriations and NAGPRA consultations have occurred in all the parks over the past 10 years and the parks have positive relationships with a variety of Hawaiian cultural and civic associations, organizations, and groups. The parks need to ensure that the documentation of NAGPRA compliance activities dealing with human remains, associated and unassociated funerary objects, sacred objects, and objects of cultural patrimony is permanently archived within the museum documentation system.

The 2001 Inventory of Museum Property for KAHO was completed for a random sample of 155 objects, none of which was lost or damaged. The inventories of PUHO and PUHE need to be updated with the assistance of a curator of record. A completed Checklist for the Preservation and Protection of Museum Collections for KAHO (2001) should be updated based upon some of the findings in this plan. No checklists were sent for either PUHO or PUHE due to technical problems.. By completing the checklists for all four parks, the identification of deficiencies and estimation of costs to eliminate them will give the parks increased justification for improving storage and obtaining the assistance of professional museum staff.

The Scope of Collections Statements (SOCS) for all four parks are in draft based upon an incomplete update begun several years ago. The former SOCS were approved in the 1980s for PUHO and PUHE. A significant update needed for all the parks' SOCS is the improvement of the definition of what natural resource collections are appropriate. The former SOCS limited specimens to one per species, or a male and female specimen per species, in order to build a reference collection. Instead, a scientific approach that emphasizes the creation of voucher and research collections based upon scientific rationales defined by the project or scientist should be developed. Thus, specimens need to have high-quality data, skilled specimen preservation, and justification based upon the need to document species diversity and abundance, as well as providing for future re-analysis and use. Specimens would not be limited by numbers per species, but instead would focus on building the scientific documentation of resources and research activities.

Recommendations

- Accession all backlog un-accessioned materials appropriate to the parks museum collections using the curator of record for assistance.

- Develop an agreement for assistance to be provided by Hawai'i Volcanoes National Park museum staff.

- Ensure that all CMRs are updated on an annual basis.

- Move all accession files to museum storage at Koloko-Honokōhou and place duplicates at the two parks for use. Place backups of the ANCS+ database at KAHO for all four parks as a method of centralized access.

- Request funding to update museum records and eliminate the backlog of un-cataloged objects and records.

- Review existing NAGPRA documentation and update/create records as necessary.

- Complete Inventories of Property and the Checklists for the Preservation and Protection of Museum Collections for PUHO and PUHE and update for KAHO.

- Update the Scope of Collection Statements. Revise the natural resource sections to reflect Inventory and Monitoring, and scientific and natural resource program rationales.

Figure 5   Pu'ukololä Heiau

Issue C – Archives and Records

Issue Statement

The successful management of records, archives, and library resources will strengthen research, promote accessibility, and support park operations.

Background

Currently, the management of museum and archival collections for the west Hawai'i parks has been assigned as collateral duty assignments for three separate permanent staff members. Very little work has been completed on identifying, processing, and cataloging archival collections and permanent park records, including resource management records and associated field records.

This may be attributed partially to the historical nature of how information resources have been managed in the past by various NPS sites. Generally, park libraries were the repositories for not only secondary source material (books and journals, audiovisual materials, etc.) but also for primary source documentation, including manuscripts, field reports, maps, slides, and photographs. Besides park libraries, the central files contained administrative records and information such as resource management records and contract files, as well as various portions of project files. Over time, park libraries and central files have both served as the park archive.

Another factor that has hampered the identification of permanent park records for the west Hawai'i parks is the lack of archival surveys and assessments. Both provide a framework to identify and locate permanent records, determine the extent of material eligible for backlog cataloging, and provide suggestions for prioritizing cataloging projects. Associated field records and resource management records are represented in numerous material/type formats such as site forms, field notes, drawings, maps, photographic prints and negatives, slides, oral histories, artifact inventories, laboratory reports, computer cards, tapes and diskettes, and manuscripts and reports. These materials are often found in various locations throughout a park including resource management offices, maintenance, interpretation, administration, and the library.

The perspective described above applies to all four west Hawai'i parks. The following information describes all known archival or records management activities that have been completed. It also provides a listing of what needs to be accomplished and in what order, and identifies any problem areas.

Pu'uhonua O Hōnaunau:

A one-day archival survey was completed in July 2001 by Lynn Marie Mitchell, Archivist from the Western Archeological and Conservation Center (WACC) in Tucson, Arizona. A total of 146,060 items were identified for inclusion in the park's museum collection.

In fiscal year 2002 the park received $20,000 in backlog cataloging funds to begin archival processing and cataloging. A team of six archival staff members from WACC completed a ten-day on-site visit in July/August to initiate backlog cataloging activities. Approximately twenty-five linear feet of central file materials were processed during this on-site visit. Storage upgrade was completed for the slide collection and 6,733 items (slides) were cataloged (PUHO #4910). The Land Files ("L") were also cataloged (PUHO #4909) as well as the Manuscript Collection (PUHO #4908) for an additional 8,400 items cataloged. A total of 15,133 items were cataloged in FY2002. The catalog records were edited at WACC and an electronic copy of the catalog records sent to the park for submission to the

National Catalog. Storage upgrade was also completed for both the Land Files and the Manuscript Collection. Approximately 50% of the central files were processed during this on-site visit. WACC staff organized the maintenance records (approximately 6.25 linear feet) and shipped them to WACC for processing and cataloging. This project will be completed in FY2003.

An additional $20,000 was made available to the park for continued backlog cataloging activities late in the 2002 fiscal year. In order to accommodate the park's need for future cataloging efforts, the funds were assigned to WACC's cooperative agreement with the University of Arizona. This was with the understanding that travel funds would be made available for two NPS employees during FY2003 (contractor's travel will be covered via the cooperative agreement.)

A review of the park library was also completed. Unique manuscript material was identified and removed for inclusion in the park archives. Copies of this material should be made for the library, but this has not yet been completed. Outdated books and training manuals were removed; duplicate materials were identified and no more than two copies were kept (primarily park-related information). Rare books were also identified. For all materials that were weeded from the library, the checkout card was removed so that the card catalog could be properly updated and accountability verified.

Additional Issues:

• Additional archival assessments are needed to ensure that all permanent park records have been identified and appraised for inclusion in the museum collection.

• A survey of the Pacific Islands Support Office should be completed to locate any additional materials that may not be at the park. Copies (either digital or hard copy) of park records should be made, particularly associated field records that may not previously have been known to exist or that would complete data sets.

• A professional librarian should review the library and assist with developing policies and procedures that will move the library program from a stagnated entity to a useable information resource.

Kaloko Honoköhau:

Very little archival work has been done. The Collection Management Report (CMR) has been amended to reflect an archival backlog of 264,000 items, based on a one-day survey that was completed in July 2001. Further assessments are needed to determine if any additional materials need to be evaluated for inclusion into the park's museum collection. These assessments are especially critical, as only collections that have been formally accessioned will be eligible for backlog cataloging funds. Like the other west Hawai'i parks, a survey and/or assessment of the Pacific Island Support Office (PISO) is necessary to locate additional park records. The park has also expressed a strong desire to begin archiving Geographical Information System (GIS) data as well as to develop a scanning program to help duplicate both textual and visual images.

Pu'ukoholä Heiau:

There has been no archival work completed. The 2002 CMR reflects an archival backlog of only 16 items, but once the accessioning has been completed, the CMR needs to be amended to include an additional estimated 50,000 items, based on a one-day survey completed in July 2001. Further assessments are needed to determine if any additional materials need to be evaluated for inclusion into the park's museum collection. As mentioned previously, these assessments are now required in order that a park may apply for BAC-CAT funds. This is a particularly important step for PUHE because it will assist with establishing accession information that does not yet exist. Like the other west Hawai'i parks, a survey and/or assessment of PISO is necessary to locate additional park records. The park should consider working with KAHO and PUHO to develop protocols for dealing with GIS data as well as implementing a scanning program to assist with duplicating both textual and visual images.

Discussion

The statistics from the pre-MMP Museum Archives and Library Survey indicate a need for improved access (both physical and intellectual) to collections as well as documentation (such as finding aids, inventories, and indexes) that will facilitate research and the use of archival collections. Twenty-six percent of those who responded to the survey use the park libraries, while seventy-eight percent use the park archives. When queried about what parts of the park collections/archives they used, 49% of the staff said they use the photo collections, 28% use administrative records, and 25% use historic collections. Responding to the primary reasons for using park archives/collections, 40% use them to complete project research, 34% to provide information for visitors, and 22% for administrative research and maintenance/repair information. When asked why they do not make use of the library, archives, and collections, the staff's primary responses were that they did not know where collections were located, did not know how to find the collections that were needed, and did not know what types of collections were available.

The west Hawai'i parks have the opportunity to develop and implement various components of an information management program(s). This should include various data systems such as GIS and Naturenotes, as well as incorporating NPS policies that concern the management of park records: DO-19: Records Management; DO-28: Cultural Resource Management; and NPS-77: Natural Resource Management. Developing such a program will help to eliminate the loss of vital park information and baseline data. Ideally, all park units should work together to develop policies and procedures that could be jointly shared and implemented. For instance, a policy on records management (which would assist in identifying permanent resource management records) is essential. This would allow for a formal program which could dovetail with archives management and systematically identify and transfer records to the park's museum collection. Such a policy should include the participation of both the records manager and the park staff that is responsible for managing museum collections.

There is a clear need for a survey/assessment of the Pacific Island Support Office to determine what records and information should be incorporated into the west Hawai'i park units' museum collections. A suggestion would be to accomplish this project after assessments have been completed for the four parks so that duplicate material is not included as part of a project. Once this project has been completed, the park units will be able to write accurate project statements for archival activities that need to be completed.

It is important to begin to coordinate the management of GIS information with that of an archive management program. This concern has been expressed by the Chief of Resource Management at KAHO and actually affects all park units. Of particular concern is management of the GIS data for the planning phase of the Ala Kahakai National Historic Trail. During this planning a records manager should be designated to begin organizing and managing this information.

The ability to provide both physical and intellectual access to collections is paramount to a successful museum collections program. Although collections may not be fully cataloged into ANCS+, inventories and indexes to various collections can be prepared to provide at least a collection level or file level access to the information. Once collections have been properly processed and cataloged, duplication projects such as scanning or microfilming should be implemented. Completion of an accurate and detailed cataloging project would also benefit the production of web sites. The duplication process would greatly enhance the ability of researchers and staff to fully utilize park resources.

Recommendations:

- Implement a viable records management program for all units, which should include administrative staff, resource management personnel, interpretative staff, and those individuals who have curatorial responsibilities. This will enable records management to dovetail with archives management.

- Survey the Pacific Islands Support Office (PISO) for additional archival materials that should be incorporated into the west Hawai'i parks' archives.

- Coordinate the Geographical Information System (GIS) with archives management at all the west Hawai'i parks.

- Designate an individual to be the records manager for the documentation generated for the planning phase of the Ala Kahakai National Historic Trail.

- Implement a system for bringing resource management records and associated information into the collections on a regular schedule.

- Prepare inventories and/or indexes for collections that will assist with providing intellectual access to staff and researchers.

- Implement a program to duplicate park records and historical collections by scanning or microfilming to provide access while protecting original materials.

- Centralize the responsibility for library management and implement the KAHO Library Policy across all park units. See Appendix C for suggested format.

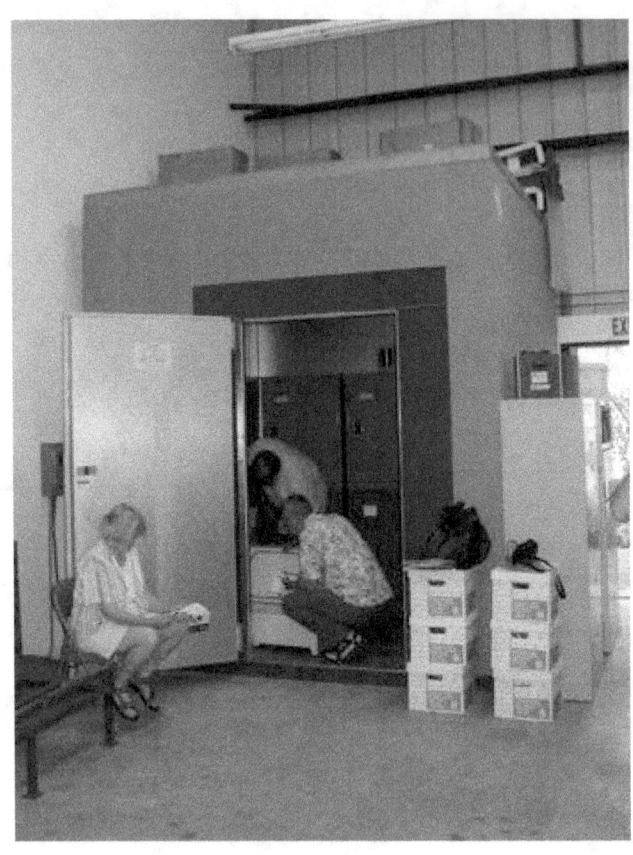

Figure 6   Bally Building at KAHO

Issue Statement

Improvements to current storage areas will ameliorate adverse conditions that impact cultural and natural resource collections until a central facility is built on the west coast of Hawai'i.

Background

Each park along the west coast of Hawai'i has an area for collection storage. All of them are inadequate for long-term care and preservation of collections and are unsuitable for public access to collections.

In some cases the storage facility was crafted out of low-cost materials, a result of inadequate funding or make-do projects. The surrounding environment affects the structures and the collections within. All four parks share common environmental conditions and face similar hazards from pests and other natural threats.

The parks share common cultural and natural themes among their collections. Likewise, the composition of the collections is similar: about 90% is archival material with the remaining 10% primarily archeological material, natural science items, and objects reflective of recent Hawaiian cultural activities. Collection growth is anticipated in all categories, but can be expected to be highest in natural science items. This growth is due to the Inventory & Monitoring (I&M) work at the parks, as well as specific initiatives such as the Coral Reef Study at KAHO, which will add significantly to the existing collection of natural history specimens and associated records.

Discussion

The four parks along the west coast of Hawai'i have at their core similar sets of issues regarding collection storage. Individually, the parks struggle to maintain minimally acceptable standards for museum management. Limited by constraints on space and hampered by a lack of staff dedicated primarily to collection management, the parks are taking steps to improve the situation. However, these steps will provide only short-term relief to the problem. It is clear that if the parks continue to operate as independent units with respect to collection management, they will continue to struggle to provide minimal levels of care for their museum collections.

Pu'uhonua O Hönaunau

The primary collection storage area at Pu'uhonua O Hönaunau (PUHO) is located at Mauka Gardens, an upland property owned by the park but not contiguous with the primary park resource area. The Mauka Gardens area is not regularly staffed, and there is no means of public access to this gated location. Two structures are on this property, one a former dormitory, the other a wood-frame constructed building that includes one large area (about 80% of the total space) for large object storage and a smaller area in the remainder of the building for collection storage.

An additional location for collection storage is within the park boundary. Here archival collections are stored in one small structure located in the cluster of administrative buildings near the beach. A reference library is kept in another building, which includes storage of some non-collection items used for native Hawaiian ceremonial events. The reference library will be relocated to the new administrative building, currently in design and scheduled for construction in FY2004. The archival material will need to be relocated to the collection storage building in the upland parcel. At this time the future location and/or management of items used for special events and ceremonies is undetermined.

The objects taking up the most space in the storage building at Mauka Gardens are *ki'i* (images). The *ki'i* are traditional wood carvings typically installed outdoors near the *heiau*. The *ki'i* stored here are pieces created as part of the park's ongoing traditional wood carving program. While some *ki'i* installed as part of the cultural landscape of the park were "retired" to the storage room after environmental damage to their bases occurred, other *ki'i* have yet to be installed outdoors.

The larger storage area housing the *ki'i* is enclosed but naturally ventilated. A small area at one end of the structure has been walled off to create a 100-sq. ft. storage room. This room is under separate lock and also has its own intrusion alarm system. Temperature control is maintained in this room by use of a wall mounted air-conditioning unit.

A free-standing dehumidifier, although not in use during the site visit, may be employed to reduce the levels of humidity in the storage room. The storage area includes a small workspace barely large enough to accommodate even one visitor/researcher. The storage room itself has six museum cabinets, a fireproof file cabinet storing collection records, about 20 boxes, and an estimated 1.5 cubic feet of file boxes.

Damage from pests is an ongoing problem for both storage areas in this building. However, the building is on a two-year cycle for fumigation with Vikane, a pesticide that is useful for treating and preventing termite infestation. Evidence of damage from silverfish, cockroaches and wood-boring ants is proof of known pest hazards at this site. Environmental damage from excessive humidity is causing deterioration of the paper-based materials. Even the accession ledger, stored in the fireproof file cabinet, exhibits foxing, a corrosive spotty discoloration on the paper.

In the near-term, an expansion has been scheduled by the park using $75,000 in repair/rehab funds to make improvements to the storage facility. It is recommended that before the storage room expansion, the adjacent storeroom with the *ki'i* receives attention. The *ki'i* need to be thoroughly documented and sorted, with decisions made on which to keep and which to remove in an appropriate manner. The long bases of the *ki'i* (which are typically installed below grade in saturated soil conditions) need to be cut off, and the *ki'i* stored in racks or upright whenever possible. The reorganization of the *ki'i* storage room must be done to provide the room necessary for expansion of the enclosed collection storage room, and must result in storage of the *ki'i* in the most culturally sensitive way possible. The reorganization of this area should also include the removal of non-collection materials. Stacks of empty movie canisters, several rusty tool boxes, an old map case, and several piles of stock wood unrelated to the *ki'i* were noted during the site visit. All of these items should be removed as soon as possible.

The expansion of the storage room should include a thorough assessment of which collections require the most care and climate control. The expanded storage room should be insulated and sealed with a vapor barrier to provide the most buffering possible from fluctuations in temperature and humidity. An improved air conditioning system is needed to provide adequate although not ideal environmental control to the expanded storage area.

A key element of the ongoing preservation activities for the collections should include an IPM or Integrated Pest Management Plan. The location of the collection storage building does not allow it to receive the benefit of regular on-going staff visits. An IPM plan and a minimal Housekeeping Plan would at the least provide a regular, documented inspection of collection storage. It would also likely reduce damage from pests or other hazards that might go unchecked.

The park should also update its Automated Checklist Program, so that the annual submission reflects actual deficiencies in collection storage conditions. The documentation of these deficiencies is a critical step in achieving priority for funding projects.

Pu'ukoholä Heiau

The current situation of collection storage at Pu'ukoholä Heiau is soon to change with the planned construction of a new maintenance facility that will include a room dedicated to storage of museum collections.

The collections are presently stored in a 100-sq. ft. area in a free-standing wooden structure adjacent to the cluster of park buildings which includes administrative and visitor service functions. Within this storage structure, about one-third of the interior space is separated behind a wall that is not solid, but does restrict physical access to the collections. Museum collections and records are housed behind the wall in two museum cabinets, one fireproof file cabinet, and a herbarium cabinet. A wall-mounted air conditioning unit provides a small buffer to fluctuations in exterior climate. However, a lack of insulation, thinly constructed walls, and inadequate equipment yields little in the way of substantial environmental control. The remaining two-thirds of the interior space of this structure is filled with miscellaneous storage of non-collection items, including supplies for park operations and special events. Additionally, the room contains items of recent fabrication that are used for traditional native Hawaiian activities and ceremonies at the park.

The design for collection storage space in the new maintenance facility includes about 10x12 storage space and a 7x10 workspace. The limited size of the storage room and the important need for access to the collections indicate that the entire space should be undivided to allow for the most flexible use for collection management activities, storage, and access. As the collection expands, so too will the need for storage and access. The space allocated to this function in the new Maintenance Building is too small for long-term needs at this park.

Since museum collections will be stored in an area providing ready access, one way of enhancing their security is to include individual locks on the storage cabinets. The reference library and archives will most likely be stored in this space as well. Items for special events or ceremonies will be stored in a separate area and not combined with museum artifacts.

The HVAC has already been cut off from the collection area and a stand alone unit will go in its place. This will avoid the potential for damage to the collection storage area from fumes or hazards from maintenance.

If at all possible, the new structure should include pipe races or channels that will permit the installation of a fire suppression system when funds become available. The new structure should include at a minimum the necessary security system and fire detection system that is most appropriate to the collections and the risks involved.

Kaloko Honokōhau

As the newest of the national park units along the west coast of Hawai'i, Kaloko Honokōhau benefits from one of the better collection storage areas. Located in the Headquarters Building outside the park boundary, collection storage is presently in a pre-fabricated metal storage unit known as a Bally Building. The Bally Building is designed to be a self-contained unit, as a structure within a large structure. The interior space of the Bally Building is roughly 8x8, and contains six museum cabinets, a fireproof file cabinet and some boxed materials. Outside the Bally Building, within the adjacent maintenance bay, are two stacks of boxes and an upright metal cabinet storing unprocessed archeological collections. Additional archival material is stored in nearby offices of the resource management staff.

The Bally Building has an independent air conditioning unit, which has been inactive for more than 18 months due to a faulty compressor. There are at present no lights inside the Bally Building, and collections and/or records are usually moved out into the resource bay when needed.

An immediate improvement to the preservation of the collections will come from repairing the faulty air-conditioning in the Bally Building. The structure itself is solid and sound, although starting to get cramped from the increasing amount of collections stored within. A light inside the Bally Building would be helpful to staff working inside, improve safety, and reduce the potential for accidental mechanical damage to collections.

The resource bay outside the Bally Building is gradually being transformed into a wet lab and prep area for archeology and for natural sciences specimens being gathered from the park as part of the Coral Reef Project.

As collections increase beyond the capacity of the Bally Building, priority may be given to those items most sensitive to environmental change and/or to those items that may require higher levels of security. In this way, prioritization will maximize the benefits of the current collection storage systems during the period before a new centralized storage facility for all four parks is constructed.

Once the combined collection storage facility is constructed, the Bally Building might be relocated to one of the other parks to store materials that may be culturally inappropriate to relocate to another area of the island.

Recommendations

- Repair the faulty air conditioning system in the Bally Building at KAHO to provide consistent environmental control for collections. Also install a light fixture inside the Bally Building.

- As collections expand at KAHO, prioritize among materials and media those collections that will benefit most from consistent environmental control.

- Prepare for the expansion of the storage room at PUHO by sorting and re-housing the *ki'i* in the adjacent space.

- Implement an IPM plan for the collection storage building, both the enclosed space and the *ki'i* storage area, to reduce potential for damage to collections.

- Determine the most appropriate means of managing the traditional items used for special events and ceremonies. If these are managed as part of the museum collection, the items should be stored with museum collections.

Issue Statement

A joint facility is required to provide protection and access for the park collections in west Hawai'i.

Background

At the present time each of the four parks has small spaces that are used to store museum, archival, and library collections. The spaces are inadequate for the current collections and do not provide work space or appropriate environmental controls. There is no professional staff to manage the museum program, and collateral duty staff assigned the work have little time in which to accomplish the required work. Each individual park does not have the workload or funding to have a professional curator or archivist. The combination of the three into one museum program would support professional staff and a facility.

In Collection Management Plans (dated 1989 based on data from 1984) developed for PUHO and PUHE, a joint facility for the parks located on the island of Hawai'i (including HAVO) was proposed. Although legislation creating KAHO was signed in 1978, the park was not established until the late 1980s, so a facility was not considered during that early museum planning process.

The General Management Plan (GMP) for Kaloko-Honokōhau National Historical Park (KAHO) proposed a park visitor orientation center to be located on the disturbed portion of the *a'ä* lava flow *mauka* (inland) of the 'Aimakapā fishpond. This facility will provide basic information and orientation for visitors to the park. In addition, "Other functions at the orientation center would be as a Hawaiian library and research laboratory; as a museum for collections related to this place and Hawaiian culture; and as a repository for Hawaiian archeological and ethnographic collections." (1994: 25-26) Throughout the KAHO GMP and the earlier study, *Spirit of Ka-loko Honö-ko-hau* (1974), there is an emphasis on the preservation and perpetuation of Native Hawaiian culture.

The four parks have done other joint planning due to the integrated nature of the resources they preserve and the stories that they are telling, including the Comprehensive Interpretive Plan (1999) and the *Historic Resources Study: A Cultural History of Three Traditional Hawaiian Sites on the West Coast of Hawai'i Island* (Greene, 1993). An archeological overview of the three parks is underway.

The National Park Service has proposed a joint facility for these four units to be located at KAHO. A project statement, "Protect Hawaiian Artifacts and Related Collections" (KAHO 4780), has been entered into PMIS which proposes a four-park facility for the preservation and protection of park museum collections. Although it was once in the Region's Line Item Construction Program for FY2004 with a priority of 2, it was bumped during the formulation for the 2002 budget because of concerns about the scope of the project and the amount of funding requested. It re-competed in 2003 and is currently Pacific West Region priority 9 in the FY 2004 – 2008 Line Item Construction Program / Additional Increment. This provides time to address the change from a five-park (including Haleakalä and Hawai'i Volcanoes) facility to one for the four west Hawai'i parks, and the proposed change in location of construction to a new site outside the park's currently legislated boundaries.

The Pacific West Region is currently working on strategic planning for the Region's museum collections. The Bay Area Museum Resource Center (BARC) in the San Francisco Bay Area and studies conducted by the Southeast and Intermountain Regions have indicated that a cost-effective and efficient way to preserve, protect, and keep museum and archival collections accessible is through centralized repositories. A centralized repository will best meet the needs of the west Hawai'i parks as well as the publics they serve.

In addition to the parks just discussed, a new NPS park unit, the Ala Kahakai NHT, was created in 2000. At the present time its headquarters is co-located with KAHO and is in the process of completing a Comprehensive Management Plan. It is expected that this planning effort will produce a great deal of documents, plans, and other records as well as the possibility of collections from the various lands that the historic trail passes through.

Finally, the opportunity to partner with a number of preservation organizations is being discussed. West Hawai'i is an extremely dynamic place with a tremendous amount of on-going development. State and federal laws require archeological investigations in areas proposed for development, as well as cultural assessments producing oral, historical, and other documentation. This development is leading to the creation of archeological collections and associated records but often the resulting collections are not accessible because of their locations throughout the State of Hawaii, as they perhaps are curated by a private CRM firm. Working with an archeologist from the State Historic Preservation Office (SHPO), the following information on current collections has been gathered:

Table 2. Summary of West Hawai'i Archeological Collections held by Archeology Contractors (numbers are in cubic feet)

FIRM	ARCHEOLOGY	ARCHIVES	TOTAL
AMEC	20		20
Bishop Museum	25		25
Cultural Surveys	168		168
Haun & Associates	27		27
IARII	50		50
PHRI	1,235	168	1,403
Rechtman Consulting	5		5
SCS	100		100
TOTAL	1,630	168	1,798

(There may be additional collections not reflected in this chart.)

Discussion

Museums face two major challenges: how to preserve their collections, and how to make them more accessible to interested parties and a broader audience. The proposed facility would combine traditional museum activities, including preservation and exhibition of collections, with more contemporary cultural center activities similar to American Indian cultural centers[1]. The facility would bring together Native Hawaiian archeology, ethnography, and natural history of the west Hawai'i area in one centralized location and enhance research and learning opportunities at all levels. It would also bridge the gap between higher education and informal learning, and invite the public to participate in the collection, preservation, and scholarship activities of museum work, as well as the appreciation of museum objects. It would allow Native Hawaiians to conduct research on their heritage and genealogy and inspire visitors to learn about Native Hawaiian culture and history. No other single investment will result in such a major improvement of the museum program for all four parks.

Having a centralized repository for Hawaiian artifacts and natural resource specimens, archeological collections, and related archival and library material now housed at the three west Hawai'i park units is the most efficient way to manage the museum collections. The proposed structure will provide the visitor with an opportunity to view all archeological collections from the west Hawai'i NPS units and to conduct research into Hawaiian Culture. Pulling together resources from the four parks will be a very powerful tool to fulfill the tenets and meet the concepts of the parks' enabling legislation.

The development of mission statements and management oversight documents to ensure all parks and any partners or other participants understand how joint management will work is a critical first step. These documents should be clear statements of the goals and objectives of the program so that all involved understand their role and the roles of the joint

---

[1] For example, Ned Hatathlii Cultural Center (Navajo – Arizona), the Museum at Warm Springs (the Confederated Tribes of Warm Springs – Oregon), and Tamástslikt Cultural Institute (Cayuse, Umatilla and Walla Walla Tribes – Washington State)

West Hawai'i Parks Museum Management
Plan

program. Legal instruments will need to be developed between the NPS and all partners and will need to be reviewed by appropriate regional staff. The program will not be just the facility but also the overarching guidance or vision for it. These documents need to be clear about how decisions are made, and the working relationships among individual park programs, staff, and other participants.

During the 19th century many important artifacts were removed from what are now parks; they are located in institutions in Great Britain, Europe, and on the mainland United States. There were also many archeological investigations prior to the creation of the parks in the 1950s and 1970s. Those collections are located in institutions such as the Bishop Museum. The SHPO has indicated that they are interested in a collections repository for archeological collections from west Hawai'i lands. This facility will create "the" repository for west Hawai'i and support re-assembling collections from far-flung sources. Other partners to be explored are:

- Hawaii State Parks Division of the Department of Land and Natural Resources.

- Bishop Museum educational facility with a garden area in Captain Cook. In recent years it has proposed a museum facility to house collections that had originated in Kona. The collection facility that it was considering would house archeological collections and items from the permanent collection of Bishop Museum that are from west Hawai'i.

- Kona Historical Society. This active group has managed to document and protect the ranching history, coffee production, and scenes of the Kona side of the Island. They have a museum, and an archive that has grown through state and federal funding. They would be a good partner in any preservation effort.

- University of Hawaii, West Hawaii Campus. All suggested campus locations are to the north of the KAHO location. The maximum distance is approximately 10 miles. The Kailua-Kona airport is 4 miles north of the KAHO location.

- Kamehameha Schools (formerly Bishop Estate). This organization has money, lands, and lots of students. They are currently promoting individual schools on each island. They own the land between the Kailua-Kona airport and the State Park at Mahaiula.

- Office of Hawaiian Affairs (OHA) and the Department of Hawaiian Homes Land (DHHL). OHA has funding, but no land whereas DHHL has both land and money. Both are State agencies.

Once these partnerships have been identified and relationships established, identification of what the partners will be providing is necessary. Support for the facility can be varied, including but not limited to, matching funds, land, staffing, and so on. This facility is an opportunity to join forces with the state and other groups to enhance protection and education programs in west Hawai'i. The strength in this project is the combination of groups which must pull together to build political, community, and national support.

Since planning for this facility is still in its infancy, projected size is currently estimated at 6,000 square feet. At the present time there appear to be several options:

- New construction, per the General Management Plan, on park land.

- New construction on land to be acquired along with the "Perfume Factory" (new KAHO administrative building).

- New construction on donated state lands or donated private lands.

- Partnering with the new campus of the University of Hawaii to be located north of KAHO.

- Rehabilitation and new construction at the site of the old YCC dormitory at PUHO (this option is not viable as there are other higher and better uses for this location).

KAHO is centrally located to the other parks and lands identified as possible donations are adjacent to the park. The new University of Hawaii campus is projected to be located across the highway from the Kona

Airport just a few miles north of KAHO. No appropriate locations have been identified on or adjacent to park lands at the other two parks.

These alternatives need to be explored more fully before a final decision is made. Other factors to be evaluated include site geology and environmental factors, availability of utilities, safety of the site, and sustainability. Undoubtedly, at least an Environmental Assessment (EA) or even an Environmental Impact Statement (EIS) will be required before implementation.

It is critical that this new facility meet the highest professional standards possible. Standards are contained in a number of NPS documents:

- *2001 NPS Management Policies*, Chapter 5: Cultural Resource Management

- Section 5.3.1.2 – Fire Detection, Suppression, and Post-fire Rehabilitation and Protection

- Section 5.3.1.4 – Environmental Monitoring and Control

- Section 5.3.5.5.1 – Museum Collections Preservation

- Section 9.4.2 – Museum Collections Management Facilities

- DO-24: NPS Museum Collections Management

- DO-28: NPS Cultural Resources Management

- *NPS Museum Handbook*, Part I: Museum Collections, Chapter 7: "Museum Collection Storage"; Appendix F: "NPS Museum Collection Management Checklists"; Appendix G: "Protection of NPS Museum Collections"

- 36 CFR Part 79, "Curation of Federally Owned and Administered Archeological Collections"

- DO-58: Structural Fire Management

- NPS Floodplain Management and Wetland Protection Guidelines

In addition, this facility should meet current National Archives and

Records Administration (NARA) standards for archival collections. Environmental standards are codified by ASHRAE (American Society of Heating, Refrigeration and Air-Conditioning Engineers). Museum collections should meet Class B at a minimum and preferably Class A standards. Finally, NFPA 101: *Life Safety Code* and NFPA 909*: Standard for the Protection of Cultural Resources including Museums, Libraries, Places of Worship, and Historic Properties* should be consulted.

This facility will provide visitors to Kaloko-Honokōhau National Historical Park and west Hawai'i the opportunity to view tangible elements of the Hawaiian culture from this and the other west Hawai'i parks. Artifacts and records from all the park areas would be stored there. The center must have access built into every element of its design and operation. This facility will include a dry/wet laboratory to process incoming objects, a library that will be accessible for those interested in the Hawaiian Culture, and space for research and education. The library will provide an archive for all documentary material related to the west Hawai'i parks and other archeological sites. It would house specimens and archival collections related to the natural resource program currently ongoing. In addition, the building will include:

- Administrative areas

- Researcher areas

- Work/processing areas

- Offices

- Collections isolation

- Conference/classroom

- Lobby exhibits and reception

- General storage

- Bathrooms/shower

- Staff break room

- Mechanical

- Receiving/loading dock

Preliminary planning indicates that the professional NPS staff at the facility would include a curator (GS-1015-11) and an archivist (GS-1420-09/11). Depending on the programs and the partners, there could be additional staff stationed at the site. In addition, archeologists, biologists, and others might work in the labs and processing areas. Project staff such as project curators or archivists would be working in the facility. Finally, interpretive and educational specialists would use the classroom and the exhibit area to provide programs to school groups and the general public. In addition, the training and education of park staff and interns in museum management would be a goal of the program to be located in this facility.

In addition to the PMIS statement for the construction of the facility, it is necessary to complete appropriate programming documents in order to implement this program. Operation Formulation System (OFS) requests for a base increase to operate the facility, including staffing, maintenance, and utilities, needs to be completed. Project Management Information System (PMIS) requests need to be made for other project-related needs such as supplies and equipment.

Recommendations

- Plan for the construction of a repository for Hawaiian artifacts and natural resource specimens, archeological collections, and related archival and library material now housed at three west Hawai'i park units: Kaloko-Honokōhau NHP, Pu'uhonua O Hōnaunau NHP, and Pu'ukoholä Heiau NHS, and for the Ala Kahakai NHT.

- Identify and contact potential partners to discuss participation in the facility.

- Develop mission statement, role and function, and management oversight documents so that all parks and others understand how joint management will work.

- Develop legal instruments to document relationships between the NPS and others who will participate in the facility.

- Complete programming documents (OFS and PMIS) to address the management and operation of this new facility.

Appendix A — Archiving Resource Management Field Records – Standard Operating Procedure

The purpose of this SOP is to aid park staff in accomplishing their responsibilities according to *NPS-77 Natural Resources Management Guidelines, DO-28: Cultural Resources Management Guidelines, DM-411: DOI Property Management Regulations, DO-19: Records Management Guidelines, 36 CFR 2.9*, and legislation associated with archiving resource management records.

The history of incorporating archival materials into the park museum collection is documented in the annual park Collection Management Report (and possibly in the SOCS). In addition, the *NPS Museum Handbook Part II*, Appendix D, documents the need for guidelines for the management of archival material. Directions are included for the retention of reports concerning both cultural and natural scientific research conducted within and for the park.

The park's archives include many unique information resources that need professional organization and arrangement to promote their most efficient use.

Park resource management staff generates records on a daily basis that should be considered for inclusion in park archives. This includes data sets, photographs, maps, and field notebooks that future generations will need to access in order to research the history of cultural and natural resource projects at the park.

Park staff is involved in capturing fire monitoring data, plant collections, air quality research, and a host of ethnographic and archeological research. Preserving the corporate knowledge of each of these individual activities depends ultimately upon the archival process. The organizing thread should be the project itself.

These guidelines are provided so future materials can be processed and included in the collection in a systematic fashion. Staff may also use this procedure for materials already in their possession in preparation for the materials being accessioned or registered by the archivist under the park museum collection accountability system, the National Park Service Automated National Cataloging System (ANCS+). Accessioning is the preliminary step in identifying collections that will later be cataloged and processed into the archives. Eventually, finding aids are created to enable staff and researchers to easily access information in the collection archives.

Staff cooperation in carrying out this SOP will greatly accelerate the rate at which materials are processed. Subject matter specialists involved in the creation of these materials carry the greater knowledge about these collections. The quality of the final product will depend upon the quality of staff involvement in the process of identifying the exact nature of archival materials.

Archiving Resource Management Field Records

Attachments A and B show, respectively, the several steps involved in archival processing of resource management materials and an example of an archival survey. Further details about the archival process are found in *NPS Museum Handbook Part II*, Appendix D. A copy of the *Handbook* is available for review from the park collection manager. An example of a park archival collection finding aid is also available upon request from the Lead Curator, PAC-WEST, 206-220-4145.

Checklist for Preparing Field Documentation:

1) Obtain an accession number from the park curator at the commencement of all new field projects.

2) Label all materials with the project accession number. Use a soft lead pencil for marking documents or files and a mylar marking pen for mylar enclosures such as slide, print or negative sleeves.

3) Materials must be arranged by material type; such as field notes, reports, maps, correspondence, photographs, etc. Each group of materials should be stored in individual folders or acceptable archival enclosures.

4) Resource management staff are responsible for turning over all project documentation to the collection manager upon completion of a project. In the interest of preserving institutional knowledge, leave collections in their original order. Original order means the organization system created by the originator of a document collection. Resist the urge to take important documents from these collections. If you need something for future use, copy it or request that the curator make a copy. After copying, replace the document or photo where you found it.   Much information about past projects has been lost because collections have been picked apart. Remember these materials will always be available. That's the whole point behind establishing an archives.

5) When the archival documentation is transferred to the collection manager, the form below should be provided. This form includes the project title, principal investigator, date of project, and a history of the project. The name of the individual who obtained the accession number should also be listed. The type and quantity of documentation would be included as well, such as maps (13), field notes (4 notebooks), correspondence (three files), and so on.

Use one copy of the attached **Project Identification Sheet** for each project.

Project Identification Sheet

Accession Number: _____ (Assigned *Only* By Collection Manager)

Your name _____

Project Title_____

Principle Investigator and position at the park during project. Please list staff who might have aided in the project implementation.

_____

_____

Researcher's office location and extension or current address, occupation, and employer or contact number.

_____

_____

_____

Type and quantity of materials in collection(s) (specimens, papers, files, reports, data, maps, photo prints/negatives/slides, computer media - format/software?) Condition. (i.e. infested, torn, broken, good) Attach additional paper if necessary.

_____

_____

Scope of Project:

Is this collection part of an ongoing project to be updated annually?   Yes _____ No_____

Research goals or project purpose, published or in-house reports to which collection relates

_____

_____

Abstract of collection content. Keywords referring to geographical locations, processes, data types, associated projects. Indicate whether specimens were collected. Attach additional paper if necessary.

Attachment A:

Five Phases to Managing Archival Collections

(From "Museum Archives and Manuscript Collections," *NPS Museum Handbook Part II,* Appendix D)

Phase 1

Gain Preliminary Control Over the Park Records
Survey and describe collections; identify official/non-official records; appraise collections and check them against the Scope of Collection Statement (SOCS); accession collections; order supplies

Phase 2

Preserve the Park Collections
Conduct the Collection Condition Survey; write treatment or reformatting recommendations; contract to conserve or reformat; re-house; prepare storage, work, and reading room spaces

Phase 3

Arrange and Describe the Park Collections
Arrange collections; create folder lists; edit and index folder lists; update collection-level survey description; produce finding aids; catalog collections into the Automated National Catalog System (ANCS+)

Phase 4

Refine the Archival Processing
Locate resources; prepare processing plan and documentation strategy; develop a guide to collections; publicize collections.

Phase 5

Provide Access to Park Collections
Review restrictions; write access and usage policies; provide reference service

Attachment B:

Sample Archival and Manuscript Collections Survey Form

(From "Museum Archives and Manuscript Collections," *NPS Museum Handbook Part II*,
Appendix D)
US Department of the Interior
National Park Service

COLLECTION TITLE (Creator/Format/Alternate Names/Accession/Catalog #s):

DATES (Inclusive & Bulk): *1850-1925; bulk 1860-69*

PROVENANCE (Creator/Function/Ownership and Usage history/Related collections/Language):
Asa Thomas (1830-1930) an American engineer, inventor, and explorer specializing in hydraulics created this collection as a record of his life, family, and employment history. Captions on some photos are in Spanish. Note: Must locate a biography of Thomas for the Collection-Level Survey Description. Check the <u>Who's Who in Science.</u> This collection was given by Thomas's third wife, Eva Bebbernicht Thomas to their son, Martin Thomas in 1930. Martin Thomas left it to his only daughter Susan Brabb, who gave it to the park in 1976.

PHYSICAL DESCRIPTION (Linear feet/Item count/Processes/Formats/Genres):
45 linear feet of papers including 15 diaries (1850-1925), 63 albums and scrapbooks, 10 lf of correspondence and 2,000 blueprints

SUBJECTS (Personal, Group, Taxonomic, and Place Names/Eras/Activities/Events/Objects/Structures/Genres): *This collection documents the life, family, inventions, instructions, and professional activities of Asa Thomas including engineering projects in the Dry Tortugas, an 1873 world tour, and hydraulic pump inventions*

ARRANGEMENT (Series/Principle of Arrangement/Finding Aid):
Into four series by type of document: correspondence, diaries, albums and scrapbooks, and blueprints

RESTRICTIONS (Check and Describe) Donor_____ Privacy/Publicity _____ Copyright _X_
Libel_____ No Release Forms_____ Archeological, Cave, or Well Site_____ Endangered
   Species Site_____ Sensitive_____ Classified_____ Fragile _____ Health Hazard_____
   Other_____ *The donor, A. Thomas's son Marvin, did not donate all copyrights. The papers are unpublished. Some inventions are patented.*

LOCATIONS Building(s), Room(s), Wall(s), Shelf Unit(s), Position(s), Box(es):
B6 R5 W2 S1-3, B1-40

EVALUATION (Check and Describe Status) Official Records __ Non-Official Records _X_
Fits Park SOCS _X_ Outside SOCS ___ (Rate Collection Value: 1=Low; 3=Average; 6=High)
Informational _6_ Artifactual _6_ Associational _6_ Evidential _3_ Administrative _3_ Monetary _1_

CONDITION (Check and Describe) Excellent_____ Good _X_ Fair_____ Poor_____

Mold_____ Rodents_____ Insects_____ Nitrate_____ Asbestos_____ Water Damage_X_
Other _____

OTHER (Please Describe)

Figure 7   Muscled anthropomorph petroglyphs in Honokōhau

Appendix B — Suggested Collections Access Policies

It is National Park Service policy that park-specific cultural and natural collections be available for educational and scholarly purposes. The Service is also charged to manage these resources for optimum preservation. To minimize the potential impact on the archives and museum collections and to ensure basic security and preservation conditions, access must be documented, restricted, and monitored. The guidelines in this appendix are followed at [*name of park*] in order to provide supervised management of park-specific resources.

Levels of Access to the Archives and Museum Collections

All serious research — regardless of educational level — is encouraged.

Providing different levels of access to collections is a standard curatorial philosophy underlying the policies of most major museums. Based on the information provided on the Research Application (included in this appendix), individuals will be provided access to different types of collections information or material depending on their needs and available staff time.

Conditions for Access

- The research application must be completed; it will be used as a basis for determining the level of access necessary, and to maintain a record of use for statistical purposes.

- Level of access will be determined by the Chief of Natural and Cultural Resource Management and/or the collections manager(s). Prior to allowing direct access to the archives and collections, alternatives such as access to exhibits, publications, photographs, and catalog data will be considered.

- Access will be made with the assistance of the curatorial staff, during regular staff working hours. A fee to cover the cost of staff overtime may be required for access outside of the normal working hours.

- Individuals provided access to archives and collections in nonpublic areas are required to sign in and out using the Guest Register.

- The Guidelines for the Use of Archival and Museum Collections will be followed by all individuals with access to the collections.

- While no user fee will be required for access to the archives or museum collections, the Chief of Natural and Cultural Resource Management and curatorial staff will determine what services may be reasonably offered and what charges may be required for services such as staff overtime, photography of specimens, or reproduction of documents.

- All photography of specimens and duplication of documents will take place on-site using the Guidelines for Photography of Museum Collections and Duplication of Historic Documents from the *NPS Museum Handbook.*

- A limited amount of space is available for researcher use of archives and museum collections. Researchers are required to check in all collections and remove all personal possessions each evening.

- [*Name of park*] reserves the right to request copies of notes made by researchers, and requires copies of research papers or publications resulting in whole or part from use of the collections.

- There may be legal considerations (such as the Native American Graves Protection and Repatriation Act, 1991) which allow or limit access to part of the archives and museum collections.

Access Policy Administration

This statement of policies and procedures is public information, and is available upon request from the following:

Superintendent
[*Name of park*]
National Park Service
[*Address of park*]

Implementation of these policies and procedures has been delegated to the collections manager(s); however, the Chief, Natural and Cultural Resources Management, has the final authority to grant access to the archives and museum collections.

The evaluation of requests should consider the motives of the researcher, the projected length of the project, the demands upon the available space, staff, and collections, condition of the materials requested, and the possible benefits of the research project. Access may be denied if thought not to be in the best interests of the resources, the park, or the National Park Service, or if use is counter to any conditions applied to the collection. It is expected that the Chief, Natural and

Cultural Resources Management, will make these decisions in consultation with the collections manager(s).

With increased attention and use, the archives and collections will require increased monitoring to provide security, to detect developing preservation problems, and to facilitate prompt treatment. Regular inventory of the most heavily used portions of the archives and museum collections will be required to ascertain object location and condition.

Research Application for Museum Collections and Historic Documents

Name _____ Telephone Number (_____)_____

Institution/Organization _____

Address _____

Date you wish to visit _____

(An alternate date might be necessary due to staffing limitations.)

Have you previously conducted research in the park's museum collection?   Yes___ No_____

Research topic and materials you wish to see

_____

Indicate which activities you wish to do

o Consult catalog cards   o Consult archeological records

o View objects in storage   o Study objects in storage

o Draw objects   o Consult historic documents

o Other _____

Purpose of your research

o Book   o Article

o Lecture/conference paper   o Term paper

o Thesis   o Dissertation

o Exhibit   o Project

o Identify/compare with other material

o Other commercial use or distribution _____

o Other _____

I have read the Museum Collection Access and Use/Research Policies and Procedures and agree to abide by it and all rules and regulations of [name of park]. I agree to exercise all due care in handling any object in the museum collection and assume full responsibility for any damage, accidental or otherwise, which I might inflict upon any museum property. Violation of National Park Service rules and regulations may forfeit research privileges.

Signature _____

Date _____

Please return to: Curator, [Name and address of park]

(reverse side: Research Application)

Park Service Use Only

Identification (provide at least one)

Institutional ID _____

Driver's License Number _____

Research Topic

_____

_____

Location of Research (check one)

o Curatorial Office

o Storage

o Exhibit Area

o Others _____

Museum Objects Reviewed by the Researcher

[NAME OF PARK]

Park	Catalog	Object Name	Location	Accession	Acronym	Number

Approved by:

Name _____

Title _____

Date _____

Museum Collections and Archives Register

[NAME OF PARK]

Date	Time In/Out	Name/Address	Purpose of Visit	Items Looked At	Accompanied By

Guidelines for the Use of Archival and Museum Collections

[NAME OF PARK]

The guidelines provided here are followed at [*name of park*] regarding use of the park's museum collections and archives. It should be noted that these resources are separate from the park's library, which is managed by the Division of Interpretation.

It is the policy of the National Park Service that its museum collections and archival resources be available for educational and scholarly purposes. The Service is also charged with managing these resources for optimum preservation. To minimize impact on these collections, it is necessary to regulate access to the materials.

Copies of the research application and the full text of the *Guidelines for the Use of Archival and Museum Collections* are available to the public, upon request from:

Superintendent

[Name and address of park]

Availability

The museum collections and archives are open Monday through Friday, from 8:00 A.M. to 4:30 P.M. Park staff should contact the park collections manager(s) for assistance with access. The museum collections and archives are "non-lending," and the materials will remain in the building.

Non-staff users must complete a *Research Application* (included in this appendix) prior to accessing information or materials to ensure that assistance is available upon arrival. Access will not normally be granted on weekends. All materials must stay within the study areas provided within the collection management facility. The size and location of these areas may vary according to the time of year, requests from other researchers, and staff available. The researcher may bring only those materials needed for research into the assigned study area.

Registration

The Guest Register, used to record access to museum and archival collections, must be signed when the collections are used by staff or non-staff members. Non-staff researchers are required to complete a Research Application (included with this policy). These forms will be retained indefinitely for statistical analysis and as a permanent record of collections use. A new application is required for each research project, and must be renewed each calendar year.

As part of the registration process, the researcher will be given a copy of these procedures to review and sign, thereby indicating his/her agreement to abide by them.

Use of Archival Records and Manuscripts

Many of the park administrative records, archeological records, and other historic reference material have been copied onto microfilm/fiche. A reader/printer is available for limited research use by the public. Where microfiche is available, it will be used for research requests. Only in the most extraordinary circumstances will original documents be used when microfiche is available.

When microfiche is *not* available, the archives user should follow these procedures to ensure careful handling of all materials:

- Remove only one folder from a box at a time. Do not remove or alter the arrangement of materials in the folders.

- Maintain the exact order of materials in a folder, as well as folders within a box. If a mistake in arrangement is discovered, please bring it to the attention of museum staff. Do not rearrange material yourself.

- Do not erase existing marks on documents and do not add any additional marks.

- Do not lean on, write on, trace, fold, or handle materials in any way that may damage them.

- Use only pencils for note-taking. The use of pens of any kind is prohibited. Typewriters and computers may be used for note-taking if provided by the researcher.

Duplication

The park will consider requests for limited reproduction of materials when it can be done without injury to the records and when it does not violate donor agreements or copyright restrictions. Depending on the number of copies requested, there may be a charge for photocopying. Fragile documents and bound volumes will not be photocopied. All photocopying of archival material is to be done by the museum staff.

Copyrights and Citations

The revised copyright law, which took effect in 1978 (Chapter 3 of the Copyright Act (Title 17 of US Code) and *Circular 15a* "Duration of Copyright"), provides protection for unpublished material for the life of the author, plus 70 years. In addition, all unpublished material created prior to 1978, except that in the public domain, is protected at least through the year 2002. Permission to duplicate does not constitute permission to publish. The researcher accepts full legal responsibility for observing the copyright law, as well as the laws of defamation, privacy, and publicity rights.

Information obtained from the park museum collections and archives must be properly cited, in both publications and unpublished papers. The citation should read:

"(object name and catalog #) in the collection of [*name of park*]. Photograph courtesy of [park name], National Park Service."

Restrictions on Use

The use of certain materials may be restricted by statute, by the creator, or by the donor. For the protection of its collections, the park also reserves the right to restrict access to material that is not fully processed, or is exceptionally valuable or fragile, and to information that may be restricted or confidential in nature.

Responding to Off-Site Reference Inquiries

It is the responsibility of the park curatorial staff to attempt to answer inquiries received by letter or telephone within at least 20 days from the date of receipt. Clearly, the extent to which this reference service is undertaken will depend upon availability of staff time and the nature of the question. The receipt of written inquiries will be acknowledged by telephone if a full response cannot be provided promptly. The staff must set time limits for answering research questions, so researchers are encouraged to use the collections in person.

A record of all research inquiries will be maintained. Such a record is useful for security and for compiling statistics on research use of the collection. Use of the collections by park staff will be included in these statistics.

Guidelines for Handling Museum Collections

Handling museum collections may be hazardous. Follow the guidelines provided here to ensure safe handling.

Archeological collections can contain broken glass and rusty metal objects with sharp edges. Historic material may retain chemical or biological contamination. Natural history collections contain chemical preservatives and possible biological contamination. Archival collections may be contaminated with mold, insects, and vermin droppings, or may contain asbestos or cellulose nitrate film.

- Use caution in handling collections, and wear gloves when requested to do so.

- Curatorial personnel will retrieve and replace material for anyone using the collections. Direct access to material may be restricted if the object is very fragile.

- Do not remove materials from storage packaging without the permission and assistance of the curatorial staff. The packaging is necessary to prevent damage and deterioration of the specimen, and to protect the researcher from potential injury.

- Always handle objects with clean hands. Use white cotton gloves when handling metal, photographs, paper, and leather objects; washed white duck gardener's gloves may be required for heavy objects.

- Do **not** use white cotton gloves when handling glass or other objects with slippery surfaces, very heavy objects, or items with friable or brittle surfaces.

- Do not pick up anything before you have a place to put it down and your path to this place is clear.

- Examine an artifact before lifting it to see how it is stored and to observe any peculiarities of its construction, fragility, etc. If an object is made in separable sections, take it apart before moving it. Do not attempt to carry heavy or awkward objects alone. Never carry more than one object at a time, and be particularly careful with long objects.

- Except for small items, always grasp an object with two hands, and grasp the largest part or body of the object. Slide one hand under fragile items as you lift them.

- If an artifact has a weak or damaged area, place or store it with that area visible.

Special Objects

- Mounted herbarium specimens should be laid on a flat surface and the folder cover and specimens handled gently, taking care not to bend the sheets or touch the actual specimen.

- Pinned insect specimens should be handled as little as possible, and then handled by the pin. Avoid bumping and strong drafts when handling these specimens.

- Skulls and skeletons should be kept in their jars or containers while examining.

- Ceramics and baskets should be supported from the bottom, never lifted by the rim or handles.

- Photographs, transparencies and negatives should be handled by the edges, and should remain in protective mylar sleeves whenever possible. White gloves should always be used when handling photographs.

- Unrolled textiles should be broadly supported from underneath rather than by holding from the edge.

Reporting Damage

Please report any damage you observe or cause to specimens.

Behavior

- Food, beverages, smoking, and pets are not allowed in the storage or study areas.

- Staff members are responsible for the behavior of any person accompanying them into the collections.

- Children under six years of age must be accompanied by an adult and physically controlled at all times. Older minors must be under the direct supervision of an accompanying adult at all times.

I have read and understand the above policy.

Name _____

Date _____

Guidelines for Photography of Collections and Duplication of Historic Documents

[NAME OF PARK]

This policy documents appropriate procedures for providing photographs of [*name of park*] museum collections, and for duplicating original historic photographs and documents. The policy is intended to prevent damage or loss through mishandling or exposure to detrimental environmental conditions.

Duplicate Photographs of Museum Collections

There are many possible uses for photographs of the items in museum collections, the most common being exhibits, publication, and research. It is the policy of the National Park Service to encourage the use of Service collections in these legitimate ventures and to make photographs of museum collections available within reasonable limitations.

Photography involves exposing often fragile museum objects to potential damage or loss from handling and exposure to heat and light. The Service minimizes this potential damage by photographing items as few times as possible. To accomplish this, the park will develop a reference collection of object photographs that will be available for public use. A minimal fee may be required for copies of the photographs.

In order to provide this service, and to build the necessary reference collection, the following procedures will be followed:

- Requests for photographs of items in the museum collections will be submitted to the park curator, who will establish any necessary priority for the work. Requests should be made on copies of the attached form.

- Requested items that do not have copy negatives will be photographed based on these priorities. A cost recovery charge for photography and processing may be required.

- Photography will be done at the park, under park control, to preclude the possibility of artifact damage or loss. The resulting photographic negatives are the property of the National Park Service.

- Once an object has been photographed, the negative will be maintained at the park to fill future requests for photographs of that objects. A minimal cost recovery charge may be required for prints.

Duplication of Historic Photographs and Documents

There is a wide variety of historic photographic processes and document types, but they all are subject to rapid deterioration from exposure to visible light and are very susceptible to damage from handling. Handling is often disastrous to these materials and causes damage such as tears, cracks, abrasions, fingerprints and stains. Handling also subjects historic photographs and documents to frequent fluctuations in temperature and humidity.

To prevent further deterioration, copies will be made of all historic photographs and documents, with the copy replacing the originals as the primary item for research and use. The original material will remain in storage, for the most part, as primary source material.

With increased requests for access to and copies of historic photographs and documents, the following procedures are necessary to establish priorities for the duplication work:

- Requests for duplicate historic photographs and documents are submitted to the park collections manager who will establish any necessary priority for copy work.

- Requested items that do not presently have copy negatives will be duplicated based on these priorities. The originals must be accessioned and cataloged into the park collection. A cost recovery charge for duplication may be requested.

- Duplication will be done at the park, or under park control, to preclude possibilities of loss or damage of the originals.

- Once the photographs have been duplicated, copy prints and modern negatives of the originals will be maintained and used for intellectual access and for further duplication. Microfiche copies of historic documents will also be maintained and will be available for use. A cost recovery charge may be required for copy prints.

The park will provide the sufficient quality duplication necessary to fulfill all the normal requirements for suitable reproduction. Outside individuals or organizations that request use of the images will be required to use only those copies provided by the park; and they will be obligated to acknowledge NPS credit if the photographs are published or exhibited to the public. By law, users must also credit the photographer, if known.

Request for Photographs of Items from the Museum Collections

[NAME OF PARK]

Catalog #	Object Name	B&W/Color	Size	Finish

The undersigned agrees to provide the following credit statement for all publication use:

"(object name and catalog #) in the collection of [name of park]. Photograph courtesy of the National Park Service."

Signature _____

Date _____

Figure 9 Ala Kahakai National Historic Trail

Appendix C — Suggested Library Operating Policy

Introduction

At [*name of park*], the curator serves as library manager and is designated as the park librarian. The libraries are an essential resource that enables staff to carry out the park's mandate. The operating policies establish guidelines and standards for developing and operating the libraries, and provide stability, continuity, and efficiency in their operation. The policies are intended to guide and support decisions of the library manager and to inform park staff and other users of the library's objectives. Operating policies will be reviewed and updated by park staff every two years and be approved by the superintendent, unless policy changes require action sooner.

Objective

The primary objective of the [*name of park*] libraries is to select, preserve, and make available material that assists park staff and site-related researchers in their work. Primary emphasis will be the support of interpretive services to park visitors.

Responsibility

Implementation of this policy is the responsibility of the library manager. This person will be designated by the Chief, Natural and Cultural Resources Management, and will be responsible for compiling a list of desired acquisitions, promptly adding new library items to the collection, shelving materials, ensuring that material is returned in proper condition, accounting for the collection, and maintaining catalog materials in computerized and physical form.

Scope of Collection

The collection consists of books, periodicals, microfilm, videotape, maps, photographs, and a vertical research file. These materials cover park mandate and development, and NPS material.

Materials in the library will pertain to the following:

(List areas of interest to the park, including cultural and natural resource management, law enforcement, maintenance, administration, and interpretation).

Selection Guidelines and Procedures

The Division of Interpretation and Education and the Division of Natural and Cultural Resources will use the following criteria in selecting materials for the library:

- Importance of the subject matter to the collection

- Authenticity and accuracy

- Permanent value and/or historic potential

- Author's reputation

- Publisher's reputation and standards

- Readability

- Price

- Availability in nearby libraries

The library manager will compile a list of desired acquisitions in August of each year. Input from all staff will be considered. Copies will be forwarded to the superintendent and team leaders for budget and reference purposes.

Microfilm

The microfilm collection will include materials unavailable or prohibitively expensive in their original form.

Periodicals

In addition to general library selection criteria, periodical selections will consider the following:

- Periodicals must supplement the collection as an additional and current source of information.

- Periodicals must occasionally or regularly publish popular articles, or historic articles of use or interest to the park staff.

Operating Guidelines

Loan Privileges

Borrowing privileges are extended to all NPS employees and volunteers at the park. There is a 30-day limit on individual loans. The 30-day loan period can be extended at the discretion of the park library manager. The library manager is responsible for reviewing the card files no less than once a month and contacting staff with overdue materials. No more than three items may be checked out at one time.

At the discretion of the park library manager or Chief, Natural and Cultural Resources Management, library privileges may be extended to the following:

- NPS employees from other areas.

- Contractors conducting research in the park.

- Researchers with valid research needs at all levels.

- Other users who will benefit the park and not interfere with normal operations.

- Non-NPS library use will be restricted to on-site use. The superintendent may make exceptions. Use of the library by non-park staff will be by appointment with the park library manager. Use will be supervised; users will sign in and check out. The library will maintain an attendance log of non-park users.

- Returned materials are to be placed in the "Return" box. The park library manager is responsible for re-shelving and re-filing materials.

No other person should re-shelve books. Materials should be re-shelved at least on a biweekly basis.

Damage and Loss Policy

Borrowers will replace lost or seriously damaged materials and, if materials are not immediately available, reimburse the park with the cost of replacement. If materials are not replaced or compensated for within a period of 90 days, a bill of collection will be issued for the estimated market value of the materials.

Abuse of library materials and privileges will result in the loss of library privileges.

Vertical File

The library will maintain a vertical file. This file contains information about the park, photocopied material not suitable for cataloging into the regular collection, pamphlets, articles, and personal accounts from diaries, journals, letters and newspaper clippings. Materials in this file will be cataloged into a vertical file index, which the park library manager will maintain. This file will be updated yearly in January.

Paperbacks

Paperbacks will be acquired for the following reasons:

- Title is not available in hardcover.

- Substantial price difference exists.

- Subject is estimated to be of current interest only.

Duplicates

Duplicate copies of heavily used materials will be acquired when needed.

Replacement

After all reasonable efforts have been made to recover lost or stolen books, replacement will be attempted if there is a demand and/or the item meets selection criteria. If possible, a replacement should be purchased by the individual to whom the lost book was loaned.

Gifts

Gifts of materials that meet the selection criteria may be accepted with the understanding that:

- The park retains the right to keep, use, or dispose of them as deemed appropriate by the superintendent.

- The materials will be integrated into the regular collection.

- Park staff will give no appraisals for tax purposes, but the park library manager may assist in the following ways:

  - Suggest sources of such information, such as dealers' catalogs

  - Provide a receipt describing the donated items but not assigning a value to them.

Controlled Access Collection

A locked cabinet will be maintained in the library with rare and fragile materials. Items will be considered for inclusion in this cabinet if they:

- are virtually irreplaceable.

- have a monetary value over seventy-five ($75.00) dollars.

- have particular historic interest to the park.

- have unusual attractiveness or interest.

- are in fragile or delicate condition.

Materials from this collection will be loaned only at the discretion of the Chief, Natural and Cultural Resources Management. Titles will be noted in the catalog as being in the cabinet. A separate list of these materials will be maintained in the cabinet.

Exhibited Materials

The library manager will compile and maintain a list of all books, periodicals, and maps that are used as furnishings and are not part of the library. The list will be kept in the controlled access area.

Interlibrary Loan

Interlibrary loans will be made only through the Pacific West Regional Library in the Columbia Cascades Support Office. Loans will be made of non-sensitive materials only, and the concurrence of the park library manager is required. The log of loaned materials will be kept.

Vertical File Policy

Items in the vertical file may be checked out in the same manner as books unless they are specifically marked to the contrary. When borrowing a vertical file, the entire folder must be taken and all materials returned to the re-shelving area.

Photocopying

Photocopying of materials is permitted except in the following situations:

- Materials could be damaged due to flattening the binding or exposure to light.

- Materials are marked "Do Not Copy."

Material photocopied for use outside the park must be labeled as follows:

NOTICE:
Copyright law found in Title 17, U.S. Code
may protect this material.

Adding New Publications

The Dewey Decimal (or Library of Congress) Classification System is used at [name of park]. The following steps will be taken when new publications are added to the system:

1. The Administration Office will receive new books and attend to all invoice matters.

2. The new books will then go to the library manager.

3. The library manager will photocopy the title page and the reverse page, and forward the copy to the Pacific West Regional Library. The library staff will catalog the book, add it to the card catalog, and prepare labels for the book.

4. The library manager will prepare an accession record for the book consisting of date received, cost, source of acquisition, and condition.

5. While books are being added to the catalog, they will be placed in the controlled access area; they can be used in the library only with the permission of the library manager.

6. The library manager will prepare a monthly memo for the park staff, listing the new additions and providing the title, author, and a short summary.

7. When cataloging is completed and labels arrive, the library manager will affix labels, pocket, and checkout card to the publication.

8. Books will then be shelved according to their Dewey number.

9. Every four months the library manager will update the park's computerized catalog with the most current copy from the Pacific West Regional Library. At this time, hard copies of the author, title, and subject listings will be added to the library reference area.

Excluded Publications

With the exception of the categories listed below, all books purchased with NPS or cooperating association funds will be accessioned and cataloged into the park library in a timely manner. Excepted categories include the following:

- Dictionaries, thesauruses, word finders, usage guides, or similar reference guides

- Other books regularly needed by employees to carry out their day-to-day duties, such as safety manuals, fire codes, regulations, laws, museum manuals, public health manuals, etc.

- Annual publications, such as almanacs, price books, catalogs, zip code guides, etc.

- Publications purchased as part of an approved training program

Books in the excepted category may be included in the collection at the discretion of the library manager.

Inventories

The library will be inventoried annually in October. An up-to-date shelf list will be acquired from the Pacific West Regional Library; the library manager will match the shelf list with current holdings and account for all missing books. Books that cannot be found will be listed on a memorandum, which will be circulated to staff for input. If this process produces no results, the list will be forwarded to the Pacific West Regional Library for deletion from the catalog.

By the end of each fiscal year, the park library manager will compile a list of acquisitions of the past year, noting source and cost. The list will be forwarded to the Chief, Natural and Cultural Resources Management.

Binding

Unbound or paperback material will be bound at the recommendation of the library manager when value, condition, or frequency of use justifies this step.

Weeding

The removal of material from the collection judged to be of no use for research or documentary purposes will occur on a yearly basis in October. Weeding will take place at the time of the annual inventory, and library managers will use the same criteria used in the selection of new materials. Items considered for de-accession should exhibit the following characteristics:

- Information outside of the scope of collection

- Outdated information

- Inaccurate information

- Irreparably damaged or worn materials

All items, including those that exhibit the above characteristics, should be carefully considered for possible historic value.

Weeding Procedure

- Items are removed from the collection following the above criteria.

- Selected material is included in a memo and circulated to park staff. Final approval of weeding is made by the Chief, Natural and Cultural Resources Management.

- A Report of Survey (DI-103) is prepared and circulated.

- Library records will be updated.

- Cataloged items are offered to the following:

  Pacific West Regional Library
  Pacific West Region Units
  Harpers Ferry
  Department of the Interior Library
  Library of Congress

Materials may be disposed of to other institutions at the discretion of the park library manager with the concurrence of the Chief, Natural and Cultural Resources Management.

The staff at the Pacific West Regional Library may be contacted with questions concerning library management or operations not specific to the parks, at (206)220-4114.

Approved by:

Superintendent:

_____ Date
_____

Chief, Natural and Cultural Resources Management:

_____ Date
_____

Library Manager:

_____ Date
_____

Bibliography

Good museum management planning requires an understanding of the library, archives, and museum collection resources as they currently exist; background on how and why these resources were developed; and information on what is required to preserve the resources and make them available for use. In order to accomplish these goals effectively, planners must first review park-specific documentation such as reports, checklists, and plans, then make recommendations based on professional theory and techniques that are documented in the professional literature.

This bibliography provides the references used in developing the West Hawai'i Parks *Museum Management Plan*. The first section gives references to park-specific documentation used by the team to understand the current status of the resources. The second section includes a list of recommended readings that will provide park staff with a better understanding of the physical and intellectual nature of these unique resources, and will enable them to apply professionally accepted techniques and standards for preservation and use.

Park Reference List

1974   Spirit of Ka-loko Hono-kö-hau
Honoköhau Study Advisory Commission Report

1989   Pu'uhonua O Hönaunau Collections Management Plan
Pardue, Nicholson, et al

1989   Pu'ukoholä Heiau Collections Management Plan
Pardue, Nicholson , et al

1996   Pu'uhonua O Hönaunau Scope of Collections Statement (draft)
Bush, Ganse

1996   Pu'ukoholä Heiau Scope of Collections Statement (draft)
Bush, Ganse

1996   Koloko – Honoköhau Scope of Collections Statement (draft)
Bush, Ganse

1994   Kaloko – Honoköhau General Management Plan/Environmental Impact Statement

1999   Kaloko – Honoköhau Resource Management Plan

1999   Pu'uhonoua O Hönaunau Interpretive Concept Plan

1999   Pu'ukoholä Heiau Interpretive Concept Plan

1999   Koloko – Honoköhau Interpretive Concept Plan

2001   Koloko – Honoköhau Museum Collections Checklist

2002   Koloko-Honokōhau Collections Management Report

2003   Briefing Statement: Kona Hawaiian Cultural Heritage Center
Nicholson

Suggested Reading List

The skills and craft necessary to perform adequate curatorial work have
expanded exponentially over the past three decades. Fortunately, the literature in
the field has also expanded to meet program needs. The current National Park
Service publications, *NPS Museum Handbook*, the *Conserve O Gram* series, and
Tools of the Trade, all provide basic guidelines. They inform the reader how to
perform certain tasks such as accessioning and cataloging, but they do not teach
the neophyte when and/or why these tasks should be done. The proper
application of the methodology presented in these documents requires a degree of
intellectual preparation and practical experience that cannot be provided in
procedural manuals or a two-week course.

The following references represent some of the best theory and practice in the
fields of collections management, exhibits and programs, and archival
management available today within the professional community. The Museum
Management Planning Team does not suggest that the park purchase a copy of
each suggested reference, but it is possible to acquire copies of these volumes on
inter-library loan.

Park managers and supervisors are encouraged to consider familiarity with the
recognized literature in the field when evaluating prospective employees or, as an
indication of continued professional growth when doing performance
evaluations. This familiarity should be a determining factor for employment at
the GS 1015/11 level and above. It should also serve as an indication of job
interest and commitment to professionalism when overall work standards are
evaluated.

Collection Management References

American Association of Museums. *Caring for Collections: Strategies for Conservation, Maintenance and Documentation.* 1984. More than 60 curators, registrars, and conservators contributed information on how to improve environmental conditions, manage inventory, register objects, and augment public use of museum collections.

Appelbaum, Barbara. *Guide to Environmental Protection of Collections.* Second View Press, 1991. Clarifies the various conditions that impact collections, how objects respond, and how to mitigate damage. Good book for the non-specialist.

Butcher-Younghans, Sherry. *Historic House Museums: A Practical Handbook for Their Care, Preservation, and Management.* Oxford University Press, 1996. This book serves as both reference and hands-on guide for all aspects of historic house management, including collections care, conservation, security, and interpretation.

Buck, Rebecca A. & Gilmore, Jean A., eds. *The New Museum Registration Methods.* American Association of Museums, 1998. This is a very well done update of the classic *Museum Registration Methods* by Dorothy Dudley and Irma Wilkinson (below). Good format and easy to reference, with up-to-date information sections concerning copyright, NAGPRA issues, and ethics.

Committee on Libraries, Museums, and Historic Buildings. *Protection of Museums and Museum Collections 1980.* NFPA 911, Boston: National Fire Protection Association, Inc., 1980. One of the best sources on fire protection and prevention, written specifically for museums.

Dudley, Dorothy H., et al. *Museum Registration Methods.* 3rd ed. American Association of Museums, 1979. Accepted as "the basic reference" for museum registrars, this classic covers registration, storage, and care, as well as insurance, packing and shipping, and loan management.

Edwards, Stephen R., Bruce M. Bell, and Mary Elizabeth King. *Pest Control in Museums: A Status Report.* Lawrence, Kansas: Association of Systematic Collections, 1980. A good guide to pesticides, their use in museums, and common insect pests.

Hensley, John R. "Safeguarding Museum Collections from the Effects of Earthquakes." *Curator*, September 1987, pp. 199-205.

Hunter, John E. "Standard Practices for Handling Museum Objects." Omaha, Nebraska: National Park Service, Midwest Region. North Dakota.

_____. "Standards for the Design, Installation, Testing, and Maintenance of Interior Intrusion Detection/Alarm System." Omaha, Nebraska: National Park Service, Midwest Region. 1981.

Johnson, E. Verner and Joanne C. Horgan. *Museum Collection Storage*. Paris: UNESCO, 1979.

Knell, Susan. *Care of Collections*. London: Routledge, 1994. Basic book on preventative conservation, focusing on specific and practical guidelines for collections care and handling.

Leo, Jack. "How to Secure Your Museum: A Basic Checklist." *History News*, June 1980, pp. 10-12.

Lewis, Ralph H. *Manual for Museums*. Washington, DC: National Park Service, Department of Interior, 1976.

MacLeish, A. Bruce. *The Care of Antiques and Historical Collections*. Nashville, Tennessee: The American Association for State and Local History, 1983. A reference for general museum collection care.

Malaro, H.C., *A Legal Primer on Managing Museum Collections*. Washington, DC: Smithsonian Institutional Press, 1985.

Metsger, Deborah A. & Shelia C. Byers, eds. *Managing the Modern Herbarium: An Interdisciplinary Approach*. 1999. Society for the Preservation of Natural History Collections. Elton-Wolfe Publishing, Vancouver, Canada. First significant publication in decades on herbaria that covers all aspects of herbaria management.

National Park Service. *Automated National Catalog System User Manual*. 1998.

_____.*Conserve O Gram*. 1974 to present.

_____.*CRM*, Volume 22, no. 2, 1999 "Archives at the Millennium."

_____.NPS *Management Policies*. 2001.

_____ *NPS Museum Handbook*, Part I: Museum Collections. 1990 (revised).

_____ *NPS Museum Handbook*, Part II: Museum Records. 2000.

_____ *NPS Museum Handbook*, Part III: Museum Collections Use. 1998.

_____.DO -19: *Records Management*. 2001.

_____.NPS-19: *Records Management Guidebook*. 1999 Appendix B (only): "Records Management Disposition Schedule."

_____. DO -28: *Cultural Resources Management*. 1998.

_____. NPS-77: *Natural Resources Management Guidelines*. 1991.

_____. DO -24: NPS *Museum Collections Management*, 2000.

_____. *Tools of the Trade*. 1996.

Reitherman, Robert. "Protection of Museum Contents from Earthquakes." The J. Paul Getty Museum Symposium on Protection of Art Objects from Damage by Earthquakes: What Can Be Done? *1984.*

Rose, Carolyn and Amparo de Torres, eds. *Storage of Natural History Collections: Ideas and Practical Solutions*. Society for the Preservation of Natural History Collections, 1992. A good "idea" book containing several photographs and graphics detailing innovative solutions to the storage of various types of materials.

_____ & C.A. Hawks, et al. *Storage of Natural History Collections: A Preventive Conservation Approach*. 1995. Society for the Preservation of Natural History Collections.

Thomson, Garry. *The Museum Environment*. 2nd ed. London: Butterworths, 1986. An excellent source on light, humidity, and air pollution.

Thomson, John, et al. *Manual of Curatorship: A Guide to Museum Practice*. 2nd ed. London: Butterworths, 1992. Possibly the best comprehensive reference in print on the craft and professionalism required for curatorial work.

Weinstein, Robert A., et al. *Collection, Use and Care of Historical Photographs.* American Association for State and Local History, 1977. One of the best basic references on this technical subject.

Zycherman, Linda, ed. *A Guide to Museum Pest Control.* The Foundation of the American Institute for Conservation of Historic and Artistic Works, and the Association of Systematic Collections. A good, basic reference on pest identification, with suggestions for methods of control.

References for Exhibits and Programs

American Association of Museums. "The Audience in Exhibition Development: Course Proceedings." *Resource Report*, 1992. A good guide to models of exhibition development; philosophy of education; learning theory; gender, culture, class and learning; spatial knowledge and its role in learning; evaluation; and visitor surveys.

Belcher, Michael. *Exhibitions in Museums.* Smithsonian Institution Press, 1992. Discusses every stage of exhibit planning, design, and presentation, including audience research and evaluation. A good resource book.

Dean, David. *Museum Exhibition: Theory and Practice.* London: Routledge, 1994. Outlines the full range of exhibition development concerns, from planning and design to evaluation and administration.

Falk, John and Lynn D. Dierking. *The Museum Experience.* Whalesback Books, 1992. Provides a good introduction to what is known about why people go to museums, what they do there, and what they learn. Guidelines and recommendations are offered to help museum staff understand visitors and their motivation for visiting.

Hooper-Greenhill, Eileen. *Museums and Their Visitors.* London: Routledge, 1994. The unique needs of school groups, families, and people with disabilities are outlined and illustrated with examples of exhibit, education, and marketing policies that work to provide a quality visitor experience.

Hooper-Greenhill, Eileen, ed. *The Educational Role of the Museum.* London: Routledge, 1994. A close look at the theories of communication in museums, exhibition theories and case studies, and educational programs in British museums, this book translates well into the American experience.

Korn, Randi and Laurie Sowd. *Visitor Surveys: A User's Manual*. American Association of Museums, 1990. A good, basic manual on how to conduct visitor surveys to accurately measure the effectiveness of museum exhibits and programs.

McLean, Kathleen. *Planning for People in Museum Exhibitions*. Association of Science-Technology Centers, 1993. Good description of the exhibition process, from planning to assessment.

New York Hall of Science. *Take to the Streets: Guide to Planning Outdoor, Public Exhibits*. 1995. Based on a series of sidewalk exhibits done in New York, this book contains checklists and guidelines for planning, designing, and implementing outdoor exhibits.

Neil, Arminta. *Help for the Small Museum*. Pruett Publishing Co. 1987. The second edition of the classic "how to" book for the development of temporary exhibits on a tight budget.

Serrell, Beverly. *Exhibit Labels: An Interpretive Approach*. Altamira Press, 1996. Solid reference tool, including discussions of label planning, writing, design, and publication. Contains very good resource list, glossary, and bibliography.

Witteborg, Lothar P. *Good Show! A Practical Guide for Temporary Exhibitions*. Smithsonian Institution Traveling Exhibition Service, 1991. The second edition of a standard reference offering practical guidance in exhibit planning, design, fabrication, security, conservation, and installation.

Archives Management References

Adela, James M. *Understanding Archives and Manuscripts*. Archival Fundamentals Series, Chicago: Society of American Archivists, 1990.

Aourada, Stephen. *Archives and Manuscript Materials in Parks of the North Atlantic Region*. National Park Service, 1992.

Association of British Archivists, Small Archives Committee. *A Manual for Small Archives*, British Columbia: Association of British Columbia Archivists, 1988.

Baird, Donald and Laura M. Coles. *A Manual for Small Archives*. Vancouver: Archives Association of British Columbia, 1991.

Bellardo, Lewis and Lynn Lady Bellardo. *A Glossary for Archivists, Manuscript Curators, and Records Managers*. Archival Fundamental Series. Chicago: Society of American Archivists, 1992.

Casterline, Gail F. *Archives and Manuscripts: Exhibits*. Chicago: Society of American Archivists, 1980 (Out-of-print).

Cook, Michael. Archives Administration: *A Manual for Intermediate and Small Organizations and for Local Government*. Folkestone, England: William Dawson and Sons, 1977.

Cox, Richard J. *Managing Institutional Archives*. New York: Greenwood Press, 1982.

Daniels, Maygene and Timothy Walsh, eds. *A Modern Archives Reader: Basic Readings on Archival Theory and Practice*. Washington, DC: National Archives Trust Fund Board, 1984.

Eastman-Kodak. *Conservation of Photographs*. Rochester, NY: Kodak publication F-40, Rochester, NY: Eastman-Kodak Company, 1985.

Ellis, Judith, ed. *Keeping Archives*. Second edition. Australia: Australian Society of Archivists and D.W. Thorpe, 1993.

Finch, Elsie Freeman, ed. *Advocating Archives: An Introduction to Public Relations for Archivists*. Chicago: Society of American Archivists, 1994.

Ham, Gerald F. *Selecting and Appraising Archives and Manuscripts*. Archival Fundamental Series. Chicago: Society of American Archivists, 1992.

Harrison, Donald Fisher, ed. *Automation in Archives*. Washington, DC: Mid-Atlantic Regional Archives Conference, 1993.

Hensen, Steven. *Archives, Personal Papers, and Manuscripts: A Cataloging Manual for Archival Repositories, Historical Societies, and Manuscript Libraries*. 2nd ed., Chicago: Society of American Archivists, 1990. http://www.archivists.org

Hunter, Greg. *Developing and Maintaining Practical Archives*. New York: Neal Schuman Publishers, 1997.

Kesner, Richard and Lisa Weber. *Automating the Archives: A Beginner's Guide.* Chicago: Society of American Archivists, 1991.

Miller, Frederic M. *Arranging and Describing Archives and Manuscripts.* Archival Fundamental Series. Chicago: Society of American Archivists, 1990.

National Archives and Records Administration (NARA). *A NARA Evaluation: The Management of Audiovisual Records in Federal Agencies. A General Report.* Washington, DC, 1991.

MacNeil, Heather. *Without Consent: The Ethics of Disclosing Personal Information in Public Archives.* Metuchen, New Jersey: Scarecrow Press, 1992.

O'Toole, James M. *Understanding Archives and Manuscripts.* Archival Fundamental Series. Chicago: Society of American Archivists, 1990.

Pugh, Mary Jo. *Providing Reference Services for Archives and Manuscripts.* Archival Fundamental Series. Chicago: Society of American Archivists, 1992.

Ritzenthaler, Mary Lynn, et al. *Archives and Manuscripts: Administration of Photographic Collections.* SAA Basic Manual Series. Chicago: Society of American Archivists, 1984.

Ritzenthaler, Mary Lynn. *Preserving Archives and Manuscripts.* Archival Fundamental Series. Chicago: Society of American Archivists, 1993.

Silverman, Cetyl and Nancy J. Perezo. *Preserving the Anthropological Record.* New York: Wanner-Green Foundation for Anthropological Research, Inc., 1992.

Swartzburg, Susan. *Preserving Library Materials*: A Manual. 2nd ed. Metuchen, NJ: Scarecrow Press, 1995.

Van Bogart, Dr. John W.C. *Magnetic Tape Storage and Handling: A Guide for Libraries and Archives.* Washington, DC: The Commission on Preservation and Access, 1995.

Warren, Susan. "Introduction to Archival Organization and Description: Access to Cultural Heritage." Getty Information Institute: San Marino, CA, 1998. On-the-Web primer includes a tutorial at http://www.schistory.org/getty/index.html

Wilted, Thomas and William Note. *Managing Archival and Manuscript Repositories.* Archival Fundamental Series. Chicago: Society of American Archivists, 1991.

Yakel, Elizabeth. *Starting an Archives*. Chicago: Society of American Archivists, 1994.